THE STORY OF
LIVERPOOL

THE STORY OF
LIVERPOOL

ALEXANDER TULLOCH

First published in the United Kingdom in 2008 by
The History Press
The Mill, Brimscombe Port,
Stroud, Gloucestershire, GL5 2QG
www.thehistorypress.co.uk

Reprinted 2008, 2009, 2010, 2011, 2012, 2013

British Library Cataloguing in Publication Data
A catalogue record for this book is available from the British Library.

ISBN 978-0-7509-4508-0

Typeset in 10.5/13pt Sabon.
Typesetting and origination by
The History Press.
Printed and bound in England.

CONTENTS

The history of Liverpool captured in a single photograph! Water Street (formerly Bank Street) was one of the original seven streets laid out in the thirteenth century. The street sign is on the wall of Tower Buildings, which now occupies the site of the fifteenth-century tower, and the Liver Building opposite is recognisable around the world as a symbol of the port in the twenty-first century.

INTRODUCTION

Humble beginnings

Imagine you are standing on the bank of a river in the north-west of England about one thousand years ago. For as far as the eye can see there is no sign of human life, apart from the smoke rising from the few fishermen's hovels that punctuate the landscape between you and the horizon. The low-flying seagulls squawk and head inland as they seem to sense the gathering storm which, as yet, is still some way out to sea. The balmy days of the last Anglo-Saxon summer are over and an autumnal mellowness hangs limply in the air. It is late afternoon and as the setting sun sinks slowly towards the skyline you are blissfully insensitive to the metaphor that confronts you. Nevertheless, you are filled with a deep sense of foreboding.

More precisely, the date is Saturday, 14 October 1066, and just under 300 miles to the south an event is taking place which will have lasting effects on the whole of the country, including the very spot where you are standing. The event, of course, is the Battle of Hastings and when it is lost and won in just over an hour or two from now, the England of old, the England in which you were born and grew up, will be gone forever. Defeated in battle by the superior forces of William I of Normandy, the England of the Venerable Bede, Alfred the Great, Edward the Confessor, and Harold II (Godwinson) will undergo changes which will completely transform the social structures, culture and language of what had been one of the richest and most influential countries in Christendom. And on the very spot where you are now standing, as a direct result of the events in the south, a town will be established which will grow into one of the major ports of the country, if not Europe. In less than 150 years' time this cluster of fishermen's huts (forming a settlement too small to even warrant a mention in the Domesday Book but occupying a strategically important position) will be granted a Royal Charter by King John. The history of Liverpool will have begun.

The Norman invasion of these islands in 1066 was the last in a long line of such visitations. The original inhabitants, the Ancient Britons, were driven back by the Romans and forced to retreat to the west and north to the areas we now refer to as Scotland, Wales and Cornwall. Then, after the fall of Rome and the withdrawal of Roman soldiers from these shores, other invaders began to cast their ravenous eyes on what Britain had to offer. From the fifth century AD the poor inhabitants of the land had to cope with and frequently accept invaders from modern Germany and Scandinavia in the guise of the Anglo-Saxons, the Vikings (or Norsemen) and the Jutes from the Rhineland. What followed was a period of some 500 years of invasion and resistance then absorption and assimilation. The original inhabitants eventually lost much of their identity and assumed the lifestyles, customs and language of the successive waves of newcomers. The result is a historical amalgam of various cultures, evidence for which is still discernable today in the place names, regional accents, dialect words and diverse architectural styles that characterise modern Britain.

But there was a geographical dimension to invasion. The Romans arrived close to the town we now know as Dover and then fought their way as far north as the frozen, rocky heathlands on the border with modern Scotland. The Saxons settled in southern England although the south-eastern part, Kent, was occupied by the Jutes. By the eighth century, the Angles and Saxons had merged into the peoples we refer to collectively as the Anglo-Saxons and they continued to occupy more and more of the country, leaving behind permanent reminders of their presence in county names such as Sussex (South Saxons) and Essex (East Saxons). The Danes arrived in the ninth century and settled a huge tract of land (the Danelaw) which included much of the eastern part of the country 'from the Tees to the Thames', and the Midlands. At about the same time the Norwegian Vikings were occupying parts of Ireland, particularly the east coast where they founded Dublin before setting sail across the Irish Sea and landing as plunderers and sea-borne bandits mainly on the Wirral peninsula between the Dee and the Mersey.

But it was not only the Saxons who left evidence of their stay in the toponymy of many parts of the country. The result of the successive invasions is that we are constantly reminded of the visitors to these shores by the place names which they have bequeathed to us: Chester, Manchester and Ribchester were all Roman settlements and are now no more than an hour or so travelling time away from the Mersey. West Derby, Bootle and Speke were Saxon settlements, many of which grew up around the north-western reaches of the country prior to the Conquest and have now been swallowed up by the urban sprawl that covers virtually the whole length of the Mersey shoreline. And the Viking Norsemen left us with names which we recognise today in places such as Arrowe, Birkenhead, Helsby and many more.

And what was happening in the south-western part of what we now call Lancashire while elsewhere history was being created by the successive invasions from Continental Europe? The answer is: almost nothing. When William sent out his commissioners in the 1080s to gather information for what would eventually be known as the Domesday Book, much of Lancashire was both uninhabited and uninhabitable. The commissioners reported back to their lord and master that much of the north-west was bleak marshland with scarcely any habitation worth noting down in their records.

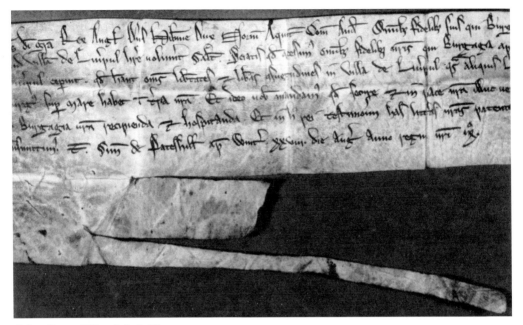

A few lines of King John's Charter.

So why did William's descendant, King John, choose this spot for his new seaport? Why did he bother to grant a royal charter* to what amounted to no more than a few miserable dwellings in a remote corner of his kingdom? In attempting to answer these questions we set out on our way through the fascinating and intricate history of one of England's greatest cities.

John's 'Charter' or Letters Patent

John, by the grace of God, King of England, Lord of Ireland, Duke of Normandy and Aquitaine, Count of Anjou, to all his faithful people who have desired to have Burgages in the township of Liverpool, greeting.

Know ye that we have granted to all our faithful people who have taken Burgages in Liverpool that they may have all the liberties and free customs in the township of Liverpool which any Free Borough on the sea has in our land. And therefore we command you that securely and in our peace you come there to receive and inhabit our Burgages. And in witness hereof we transmit to you these our Letters of Patent. Witness Simon de Pateshill at Winchester on the twenty-eighth day of August in the ninth year of our reign.

* Signed 28 August 1207 in Winchester John's 'Charter', written in Latin, was really a type of deed known as 'letters patent'.

WHAT'S IN A NAME?

Let us begin at the beginning: the name Liverpool. Historians and linguists alike have struggled over the years to come up with a definitive explanation for the origin of the name. Many theories have been put forward, some of which are probably on the right track and may, as our knowledge increases, guide us to a definitive answer. But other theories say more about the inventiveness and imagination of those who advance them than the reliability of their powers of etymological deduction.

One theory which is easy to discount, for instance, is that the name is somehow related to the word 'laver', a kind of edible seaweed which is supposed to grow in abundance along the Mersey shoreline. It may grow in abundance there, but it could hardly be the origin of the place name as the word 'laver' was not recorded in English until the sixteenth century. If at some future date it can be proven that the word did indeed exist in English earlier than we thought we might have to revise our theories, but for the moment at least, it seems safe to discount this association.

Nor is there any connection between the name Liverpool and the so-called Liver Bird. Most authorities now agree that this ornithological wonder is nothing but a myth, which most likely arose from a combination of error and confusion. When John granted his charter he marked the authenticity of the document, as was the custom in those days, with his seal the design of which included a prominently displayed eagle. As this eagle was copied by hand over and over again down the centuries the bird began to look less and less like an eagle until its shape and form could not be attributed to any known avian species. But as the bird, of increasingly indeterminate form, was inextricably linked in people's minds with the new borough it came to be known as the Liver Bird. Any claims that the city is named after this or any other extinct bird, are, at best, spurious.

We know that when the Domesday Book was being compiled the town simply did not exist. Warrington, Chester, West Derby and other settlements we now consider to be of less importance than Liverpool were mentioned, but the few huts and hovels clustered along the shore of the Mersey were totally ignored.

Why the 'Domesday' Book?

There are two theories concerning the origin of the term Domesday. According to one the word was just a popular, humorous title used by people to describe the official record of land and property in England (excluding London, Winchester and Northumbria) drawn up on the orders of William the Conqueror.

According to this theory, the similarity with the word 'doom', meaning fate, ruin, and destruction was no accident. It was assumed that the wits who coined the phrase were pointing out that once your lands and possessions were set down within its pages you had as much chance of avoiding taxes as you had of escaping your fate on the Day of Judgement.

Advocates of the second theory maintain that the word is a corruption of the Latin *Domus Dei* (the House of God) as the book was originally kept in the Domus Dei chapel at Westminster (although some say it was at Winchester).

Then, as if by magic, after 1089 we start to find references in contemporary documents to a settlement variously recorded as Lytherpool or Lyrpool. In the time of Henry II (1133–89) another spelling, Litherpool, appears, and by the time John (1167–1216) came to the throne its written form was Lyrpul. After this we have a succession of spellings: Liverpolle, Liverpull, Lierpull and Lyerpull, until, in Henry VIII's time, we also find Lyrpole or Lyverpoole. Then came Leverpool and eventually Liverpool.

However the first element of the word is spelt, there is much room for discussion on its meaning and derivation. The most commonly held opinion among historians is that the derivation of the name is the Anglo-Saxon word *lifrig*, meaning 'clogged' or 'coagulated', and the assumption here is that the original settlement acquired its name from the Mersey inlet which in ancient times was reputed to be choked with weeds and silted up with alluvium washed down from the Pennines. This is a distinctly plausible explanation, apart from the lingering doubts of both a practical and geographic nature that might trouble the linguist, if not the historian.

The main reason King John took a liking to the place was that it would make a good, sheltered harbour for his navy. Sheltered it might have been, but would a king looking for a suitable haven for his ships choose a creek that was clogged up for most of the year? Surely such an anchorage would either hamper the free movement of ships or would be prohibitively expensive to keep clear. Just think about it: the tiny sailing vessels were totally at the mercy of the winds and it is extremely unlikely that John would have wanted the additional problems associated with a shallow creek which could snarl up his navy even when the wind was favourable. If we add to this the fact that his quest for a new port was driven by his need to transport his armies to Ireland, things start to look even more complicated and improbable. A vessel of the type at the king's disposal in the thirteenth century, loaded with crew, soldiers, horses, victuals, bales of hay, barrels of fresh water, armour and weapons, would have lain heavy in the water and been even more difficult to manoeuvre out of a 'clogged' creek.

The suggestion that *lifrig* meant 'coagulated' is even more bizarre. The dictionary definition of 'coagulated' is 'semi-solid; curdled', so if the muddy contents of the creek were so dense that they could be described as 'coagulated' it is unlikely that John would have considered it as a possible future harbour for his ships. Any vessels that found themselves, either by accident or design, in a 'coagulated' harbour would be going nowhere.

From a purely geographical point of view, the idea of the Pool being 'clogged' also looks doubtful. We know that the Mersey has some of the strongest tides in the country and that it gets a good flushing twice a day from the ebb and flow of these tides which, at certain times of the year, can raise the water 9ft in one hour. Add to this the historical evidence that the Mersey once teemed with salmon, a fish that needs fast-flowing, clean and well-oxygenated water, and we arrive at only two possibilities: either the Pool was totally unaffected by the rapid Mersey tides (which seems highly improbable) or the Anglo-Saxon word *lifrig* is not the origin of the first part of the name Liverpool. But there is the indisputable evidence that the Pool was indeed affected by the tides just as the Mersey was and is. Thomas Steers, the engineer who was appointed to oversee the filling-in of the Pool in the eighteenth century, found the tidal flow of the Mersey so strong that he had to construct enormous floodgates to hold it back. And more recently, in 2001 to be exact, during excavations of the old dock, archaeologists found that their trench still filled up and emptied with seawater as the tide ebbed and flowed. So how did we arrive at the conclusion that the name of Liverpool is derived from the Anglo-Saxon word *lifrig*? The word is in fact the adjective from the noun *lifer* 'liver' and so meant 'liverish' or 'liver-like' and could have been a reference to the dark, inky colour of the Mersey, which just might have reminded our ancestors of the bile secreted by the anatomical organ. But again, this explanation does not sit comfortably with the fast-flowing clean and well-oxygenated waters needed for salmon to thrive.

So let's consider another possibility. We know that from the year 902AD the territory surrounding the Mersey saw Viking invasions and settlements and many of the place names so familiar to us today in that part of the world are Norse in origin. A quick glance at the map of the North-West of England will reveal places with names such as Toxteth, Aigburth, Thingwall, Kirkdale and many more which bear testament to the unbidden guests who left their mark on the area. So any theory which includes the possibility that it was the Vikings and not the Anglo-Saxons who came up with the original name for the humble fishing hamlet on the banks of the Mersey has to be given serious consideration.

We saw above how one of the earliest (possibly the earliest) spellings of the place name was 'Litherpool' or 'Lytherpool' and this might just be our best clue in our trying to discover the origin of the name. 'Lith' or 'Lyth' as a place name element can be seen in another Norse settlement, Litherland, a little further along the coast from where Liverpool now stands and it is not unreasonable to suggest that the two places might be connected etymologically. 'Lith' (and its alternative spelling 'Lyth') is derived from the Old Norse *hlith* meaning 'slope' or 'hillside' and so it is quite possible that the Viking invaders had identified two coastal settlements which shared a similar geographical feature: one was the place where the land 'sloped' down to the sea and the other was where it 'sloped' down to a creek or pool.

The second element in the word Liverpool is quite straightforward. It is derived from the Late Latin *padulis* which originally meant 'marsh' but made its way into English and changed its meaning slightly so that it now means a small body of water.

Meanwhile, elsewhere . . .

1070	Hereward the Wake leads rebellion in the Fen country
1087	Death of William the Conqueror
1096	First Crusade begins
1147	Second Crusade begins
1162	Becket becomes Archbishop of Canterbury
1170	Becket murdered in Canterbury Cathedral
1190	Third Crusade begins
1199	King Richard dies and John becomes king

2

LAYING THE FOUNDATIONS

It appears that Liverpool owes a lot to pure chance. The story goes that King John needed a suitable port of embarkation for his troops, as the rebellious Irish were causing him a good deal of trouble and he had decided to send his army across the sea to teach them a lesson. Unfortunately, Chester, which had until then always been the principal port serving the north west, was no longer thought to be as reliable as it had been in the past. For a start it was in the hands of a semi-autonomous earl who could be less than cooperative if he felt like it. Secondly, Chester was more or less on the border with Wales and the Welsh had no particular liking for the English either and were more than capable of making things very difficult for them if they chose to. So, all in all, Chester was vulnerable for several reasons and John was keen to find an alternative.

The story continues that on one of his very rare trips to the distant northern regions of his realm (actually Lancaster) some of his entourage suggested that he might like to cast his eye over a certain inlet which they had discovered not far from Warrington. As this was the spot where he was going to have to cross the Mersey anyway, it was not much of a detour and the inlet might prove to be just what he was looking for. And it was; it was perfect. The decision was made and he set about making plans for the creation of a new borough.

As we have already seen, there was no settlement worth mentioning on the banks of the Mersey when the Domesday Book was compiled. However, we do know that much of the territory in this part of the world formed what was known as a 'berewick' or subsidiary farm of the ancient Saxon manor of West Derby.

John has never had a good press. History (and Hollywood) has always portrayed him as the evil brother of King Richard ('the Lionheart') who is painted as the valiant defender of the rights of all Englishmen. John's seizure of the throne while Richard was held captive in Germany has never done his reputation any good and nor has the fact that he arranged for his own nephew's murder (Arthur) whom Richard had nominated as his successor.

Just how much of this is an accurate picture of the brothers is difficult to say since opinions among historians differ as to their respective characters and suitability as Kings of England. What we can be reasonably sure of, however, is that John was probably not as black as he was painted and Richard certainly was not as white.

John was the youngest son of Henry II and Eleanor of Aquitaine and during his lifetime he acquired two nicknames: 'Lackland' and 'Softsword'. The former was a reference to the fact that he did not inherit a large fief from his father as his brothers had done, and the latter because of his disastrous showing in the war of 1203–4 against Philip of France when he lost Normandy, Anjou, Maine, Touraine and most of Poitou and returned to England with his tail between his legs. He could be cruel and dictatorial, particularly when it came to squeezing his subjects for more and more taxes, but he lacked backbone and had no stomach for war. In a disagreement with the Pope over whether or not Stephen Langton should be Archbishop of Canterbury, his initial displays of bravado were followed by eventual submission and abject capitulation. In 1209, the Pope excommunicated him for his refusal to appoint Stephen Langton to the highest ecclesiastic position in the land and although John resisted for a while he was eventually forced to back down in 1213.

Of course, history remembers John mainly for his signing of the Magna Carta (the Great Charter) in 1215. But this was not a great act of genuine concern for the plight of his subjects, far from it. It was another instance of his bowing to pressure, this time from his barons who had reached the end of their tether over the crippling taxation which he had attempted to foist upon them. Reluctantly, John signed the document and simultaneously signed away many of the feudal privileges he and his forbears had hitherto enjoyed.

Mersey and Mercia

The place name Mercia is derived from the Anglo-Saxon 'mearc' meaning border and is so-called because it stretched all the way from the east coast to the borders with Wales.

The same linguistic root provided the name for the River Mersey which was originally made up of two Anglo-Saxon words, 'mearc' (border) and 'ea' (river). The reference here is to the fact that this stretch of water formed the boundary between Mercia and Cumbria, which, in Saxon times, included what we now know as Lancashire.

The Anglo-Saxon 'ea' is derived from the Latin 'aqua' (water) and is thus cognate with other continental and British place names such as Aix-en-Provence, Aix-la-Chapelle (in which 'aqua' has evolved into 'aix') and the Roman name for Bath, Aqua Sulis.

John's first problem when he decided to create a new port and borough in this part of Lancashire was that the land did not actually belong to him. His father, Henry II, had made a gift of the little hamlet and surrounding land to Warin, the constable of Lancaster castle, and these were now in the possession of his son, Henry, by this time termed Fitzwarin. There appears nothing to suggest that the king and Henry Fitzwarin were unable to come to an amicable arrangement and John became the proud owner of the land in exchange for other property elsewhere.

The hamlet and surrounding area were actually within the parish of Walton, some four miles inland, which, along with many other places which we now think of as suburbs of Liverpool such as Woolton and Everton and many more, were in reality old Saxon settlements. So, once he had decided to create a new borough, he was faced with the problem of how he was going to plan it and then persuade people to come and live there. And this is where his planning ability came to the fore and perhaps made up somewhat for his otherwise unenviable reputation. He quite simply let it be known far and wide that he was inviting people to come to the area and take up 'burgages' or plots of land which could be cultivated and each of which would include a humble dwelling in which the 'burgesses' (as these new settlers would be known) could house their families. Just how many there were to start with we have no way of knowing, but we do know that by 1300 their number had reach 168.

Walton

The name tells us that at some point in history this must have been a settlement inhabited by Celts, even though we think of it as being a Saxon village. Originally the name would have been 'walas ton', the second element, 'ton', being from the Anglo-Saxon 'tun', meaning enclosure, farmstead or manor. The first part of the name, 'walas' was the Anglo-Saxon for 'foreigners' but was used particularly to describe the Celts. Also derived from this word are 'Wales' (a place where foreigners live) and even the humble 'wallnut', which really means nothing more than 'foreign nut'.

But there was an additional incentive. Prior to 1207, most of the peasantry in the area were feudal vassals living on lands owned by the Lords of the Manor of West Derby and totally in thrall to them. Part of everything they grew they had to surrender to the manor; they could not move away or get married without the Lord's permission and were obliged to grind their corn in his mills and pay an appreciable sum for the privilege. But John offered them something different. If a peasant wanted to get involved in his grand enterprise he could take one of the burgages, pay a rent of 1s per year and that was that. There was nothing more to pay and no further allegiance expected. He tilled the land, grew the crops, fed his family and sold his produce at market; he was no longer a serf of the local landowner. And, furthermore, it became the law of the land that any serf who escaped from his master, obtained a burgage and lived as a 'Pool' burgess for a year and a day was henceforth a free man. His former lord and master could no longer lay any claim to him.

West Derby

What is the correct pronunciation of the word 'Derby'? Among people who like to think of themselves as educated or refined, it is pronounced as if it were spelt 'Darby'. Many Scousers, on the other hand, insist on pronouncing it as it is written, and they are probably right!

The word 'derby' is an Anglo-Saxon combination of the words 'deor' and 'by', meaning 'deer' and 'homestead' respectively. But in Anglo-Saxon the word 'deor' meant any animal or beast (as does its cognate in modern German, 'Tier') and would have been pronounced more like 'der' than 'dar'.

When he came to working out what shape his new borough would take, John seems to have had but one thought in his mind: keep it simple. And it worked. He laid out a basic plan consisting of no more than seven streets arranged roughly in an 'H' formation, and these have remained the nucleus of the town right up to the present day.

The present-day Strand (Old English for 'shore') follows the original shoreline of the Mersey and it can be safely assumed that John took this as his starting point. The road we now call Water Street led up from the water's edge (although it was originally known as Bank Street as it formed a 'bank' leading down to the water) until it came to the other thoroughfares we now know as Castle Street, Dale Street, Tithebarn Street (formerly Moor Street), Old Hall Street (formerly Whiteacre), and High Street (formerly Juggler Street). Parallel to Water Street is the last of the original streets, which we now call James Street.

It may seem almost impossible to imagine now, when we look at a map of modern Liverpool or wander through its myriad streets, avenues and roadways and gaze at the houses, office blocks, museums, libraries, statues and monuments that for most of the Middle Ages these few streets laid down by King John were all that there was of the borough. This was little more than what we should think of today as a tiny market-town-cum-fishing-village. John is credited with not only founding the borough, but also starting the weekly market and annual fair to be held every year on St Martin's Day, 11 November. On any day of the week, but particularly on market days, farmers would have been seen driving their cattle and swine along modern Castle Street and fishermen would have called out their wares from open stalls clustered around today's Town Hall. And we know from records of the time that those who caught and sold fish probably made quite a respectable living. Fish was plentiful and the different varieties on sale would do any modern fishmonger proud: skate, salmon, fluke, lamprey (considered a delicacy in the Middle Ages) cod, mullet, perch, carp, haddock and mackerel were just some of the fish available to the good people of the new borough. And we also see from contemporary records that a particularly plentiful fish must have been the herring because, alongside 'fishmongers', the records also speak of 'herringmongers' who, presumably, could survive reasonably well by selling nothing else but this humble culinary delicacy.

It has to be said, however, that John's motives in setting up the market may not have been entirely altruistic. Obviously he probably used it as an additional attraction to entice people to move into the area, but he would also have had an eye to the profit he could make personally from such an enterprise. His burgesses paid no taxes, but 'foreign' tradesmen (i.e. those from outside the borough) had to pay whatever taxes the bailiffs could extract from them. He also introduced a shipping tax to be paid by any ships using the port; he established a special court known as the Portmoot, which the burgesses were obliged to attend at least twice a year, where miscreants would have been required to pay fines of varying severity. He is also thought to have been responsible for the building of a flourmill somewhere in the vicinity of what is now Tithebarn Street. John also appointed certain market officials whose responsibility was to make sure that everything ran smoothly and that all taxes due were paid. There were the bailiffs, as we have already seen, but there were also officers known as 'levelookers' and 'praysers' who were tasked with assessing the nature and quality of the wares offered for sale by the 'foreigners'. He also appointed a 'hayward' whose job it was to supervise the Townfield, the area to the north of modern Tithebarn Street, paying particular attention to the fences and hedges. These had to be kept in good order to make sure that the pigs and cattle did not damage the crops as they were being driven to and from market.

Hayward

The term 'hayward' would have originally been known in Anglo-Saxon times as a 'haga waerd', literally the 'guardian of the haga' or piece of land owned by a private citizen. This land would normally have been delineated by a hedge and over time the noun came to apply to the surrounding fence rather than the piece of land itself. A further derivation of 'haga' is 'haw', which is why we now have the hawthorne bush.

The Anglo-Saxon word 'haga' survives in a slightly altered form of 'hey' in the street names around Tithebarn Street: Hackin's Hey, Tempest Hey and Lancelot's Hey. And then of course, a bit further out from the centre, there is the famous children's hospital known as Alder Hey. Possibly the name refers to a piece of land that was once surrounded by an alder tree hedge.

But the tradesmen and their customers did not just want to concern themselves with the mundane affairs of survival. When they had sold their wares or bought their provisions they wanted a certain amount of relaxation. No doubt they would call in to one of the many alehouses that were hard by the market and perhaps stay and watch the strolling players and street entertainers in Juggler Street (modern High Street, right next to today's Town Hall). Presumably he would have kept a wary eye out simultaneously for the pickpockets and footpads who would have mingled with the crowd just as their counterparts did in any other market in medieval England.

Juggler*

Nowadays the word juggler suggests an entertainer who can keep several objects in the air simultaneously, but originally there was a bit more to this kind of spectacle. At the time, when Juggler Street was set aside from the market for the purposes of entertainment, a juggler would have been expected to do far more than just keep three or four balls in the air at once. He probably did a bit of what we now refer to as juggling but his prime role was to make people laugh. In fact, the etymology of the word suggests that he was in all probability closer to what we would now think of as a stand-up comedian. The origin of the word is Latin 'ioculari' meaning 'to speak in a humorous manner'. A derivative of this verb was the noun 'iocus' which is the origin of the modern English word 'joke'. Another associated word, 'ioculator', 'one who tells funny stories' passed into Old French as 'jongleur' and this then made its way into English as 'juggler' and then changed yet again into the form we now recognise as 'joker'.

King John died in October 1216 at the age of 49. His death was as unheroic as had been much of his life. Louis of France had invaded England earlier in the year and was making his way northwards after being welcomed by the inhabitants of London. John marched out to meet the invader but got caught by the incoming tide as he was crossing the Wash in Lincolnshire. All his belongings and caskets containing the crown jewels were sucked down into the quicksand, never to be seen again. Soon afterwards John became ill (some say through over-eating) and died at Newark in October. He was little mourned, but he has gone down in history as the man who laid the foundations both of the English constitution and the borough of Liverpool.

Meanwhile, elsewhere . . .

1204	Crusaders capture Constantinople
1204	Death of Eleanor of Aquitaine
1207	Future King Henry III born
1213	Foundation of St Thomas's Hospital, London
1214	William the Lion of Scotland dies and Alexander II becomes king
1215	Llewellyn captures Abergavenny Castle

* For a fuller discussion of the word see *Word Routes* by Alexander R. Tulloch, Peter Owen, 2004

3

THE MIDDLE AGES

When John died suddenly and unexpectedly his son was only 9 years old and it wasn't until 1227, when he reached the age of 20, that he assumed the throne as Henry III of England. By all accounts he grew up to be a polite and cultured young man who was good company with a ready wit, a natural sensitivity and more than just a modicum of feeling for the arts. It was Henry who, for perhaps both religious and artistic reasons, added the eastern section of Westminster Abbey and gave the country a permanent reminder of his interest in architecture.

But there was another side to his character. He appears to have been very reluctant to crack the whip and simply lacked those qualities of leadership needed for imposing his will on strong men. Nor was he a very good judge of character and years of domination by Hubert de Burgh, his tutor in his formative years, left him virtually incapable of imposing his will on his subordinates.

And he demonstrated other character defects as well which were to prove unfortunate for the country and disastrous for Liverpool. He was hopelessly inept when it came to organising either his own or the country's finances and this, combined with his inability to choose his friends wisely, led him to make decisions which at best can be described as unwise. For a start he struck up a friendship with a certain Peter des Roches, a native of Poitou in France, who took advantage of the King's beneficence and appointed his Poitevin friends and cronies to some of the most important royal and administrative positions in England. Such behaviour caused a good deal of resentment among Henry's subjects.

As if this were not enough, he then married Eleanor of Provence (1236) and this led to another influx of foreigners from Savoy and Provence who cashed in on the marriage and were able to receive revenues which the King's native subjects felt were rightfully theirs.

These moves might be written off perhaps as the foolish mistakes of youth, but they were compounded by the political manoeuvrings and financial demands made by those outside Henry's realm and over which he had little or no control. The Pope (Gregory IX), for instance, began sending requests for money (actually he demanded one-tenth of the wealth of the English laity and clergy) to help him in his campaign against the Emperor Frederick. The King refused, but this did not prevent him from finding some other way of spending the money which he did not really possess. At some point he began nurturing vain hopes of retaking much of the territory of France, and as a result soon found himself at war with Louis IX. For several reasons, not least of which was the fact that his barons failed to support him, he lost the war and so was even deeper in debt than ever. As a temporary means of lessening his financial burdens he turned to his barons for scutage (sums of money paid by holders of the knight's fee in lieu of military service), which seems to have been paid grudgingly.

This was the kind of man who ruled the country and who, as it turned out, was no friend to Liverpool. From almost as soon as he came to the throne the spendthrift Henry was looking for ways to raise money. And one of the ideas he came up with was to grant Liverpool another charter, but for the privilege the burgesses would have to find the enormous sum of £6 3s 4d. In return for this vast sum of money, Liverpool burgesses were granted a charter which allowed them to elect their own officers and settle problems relating to property in their own portmoot. They would also be free of all tolls, not just in Liverpool but throughout the land.

This might seem like a generous act but there were some pretty stringent conditions attached. Not only did Henry's coffers swell to the tune of the original payment but he also continued to receive tolls from strangers coming into the borough for markets and fairs, the fees and fines paid in the portmoot, profits from the flourmills and from the Mersey ferry.

All these taxes and fees were collected by the King's sheriff until the burgesses decided they would rather take on the responsibility themselves and asked the King to accept a further £10 to get rid of the sheriff. Unsurprisingly, Henry accepted. £10 was too much to refuse and he was still going to receive a steady income in taxes etc. from the Liverpool burgesses. What he agreed to was an arrangement known as a 'fee farm' lease, which meant that the burgesses could fix and collect the taxes from the farms and lands independently of the King's officers but he, the King, would receive a fixed sum to be paid directly to the Exchequer. It seemed to work well. Everyone was happy and the arrangement suited both sides. But then Henry had other ideas.

Sheriff

The word is a compound of two Old English words. 'Scir' meaning 'business' 'administration' and then by extension 'an administrative area' or, in Modern English, a 'shire' combined with 'reeve' giving 'shire reeve' which contracted into 'sheriff'. The ' reeve' was originally a master or commander of a troop of soldiers and he took his title from the Old English 'refan' 'to call' or 'to summon', as his primary task in an emergency was to 'call out' his body of men.

Henry needed money, but he also needed friends in high places, and so, just seven months after coming to an understanding with the burgesses of Liverpool, he suddenly granted all his lands in Lancashire to Randle Blundeville, Earl of Chester and thus, on a royal whim, the status quo was revoked and Liverpool fell under the control of the earls.

For the next 170 years the history of Liverpool is largely the history of the relationship between the good people of Liverpool and a succession of earls whose attitudes to the borough varied considerably. When Randle Blundeville died, control passed first of all to his brother-in-law William de Ferrers, Earl of Derby, and then to his son, also William, and finally to William's son, Robert. Unfortunately, Robert was something of a hothead and he sided with Simon de Montfort in the Barons' Revolt, and when he was defeated and killed at the battle of Evesham in 1265 the lands were granted to Henry's second son, Edmund, Earl of Lancaster.

While the land belonged to the Ferrers family the burgesses of Liverpool fared reasonably well. The evidence seems to indicate that neither William nor Robert interfered too much with the affairs of the town and when the fee farm agreement came up for reconsideration they renewed it without any increase in the fees due to them. William de Ferrers even built a castle (1232–7) at the end of what is now Castle Street on the site occupied by the Victoria Monument.

The Victoria Monument occupying the site of the old castle.

But things were very different under the Earls of Lancaster. Edmund saw the borough as little more than a source of income and he trampled on the rights granted to the burgess by the previous charters without so much as a by your leave. But when Thomas took over things seem to have got even worse and it was not until Liverpool passed back again under royal control during the reign of Edward II (1307–27) that things started to improve for the borough. And improve they certainly did, despite the fact that the period was characterised, not only in Liverpool but throughout the country, by violence and lawlessness on a scale not known before during peacetime. The burgesses now regained many of their former privileges, and when Edward III (1327–77) came to the throne the port of Liverpool went through a period of rapid commercial expansion.

Edward's reign was a time of almost continuous war. He fought the French, the Scots, and the Irish, and in the case of the latter two Liverpool was indispensable. King John had seen the possibilities for Liverpool as a viable port of embarkation for his troops, but it was Edward who really took advantage of the strategic position the town occupied. Troops were transported through Liverpool on their way to Scotland and Ireland in their hundreds, and the main beneficiaries, from a commercial and financial point of view, were the people of Liverpool.

The troops would muster in their camps all around the outskirts of the borough, probably on land now occupied by St George's Hall, Lime Street and Lime Street Station, as they awaited embarkation. And it is not unreasonable to expect that they would have frequented the taverns and alehouses of the town and bought their victuals and supplies from the butchers, the bakers and the candlestick makers in the thriving town centre, a mere leg-stretch away from their encampment. We know from records of the time that local cottage industries included tanners, drapers, tailors, boot-makers and souters (leather workers who specialised in the making of jerkins and saddles). But the most important industry was almost certainly brewing. Of the 197 houses that comprised fourteenth-century Liverpool, giving a total population of approximately 1,200, no fewer than eighteen were directly involved with the brewing of ale. Trade, in short, was booming and many of the commercial connections forged with Ireland during Edward's wars were maintained after the end of hostilities and thus the basis of Liverpool as a trading community was well and truly established.

But the period also saw changes in the way the town was administered. Hitherto the chief officials of the town were the two bailiffs, one of whom was elected by the burgesses and the other by the Lord of the Manor. The more important of the two was the Lord's bailiff, the *major ballivus*, but over time his authority diminished as the burgesses had gained almost all the rights of self-determination. They therefore took it upon themselves to elect their own *major ballivus*, a term which was eventually shortened to *major*, the origin of the word 'mayor'. And the first Mayor of Liverpool was William, son of Adam of Liverpool, elected to the post in 1351.

Bailiff

This is a good example of how words can pass from one language to another and in the process change from designating rather humble social status to being used with reference to more elevated positions.

The Latin word from which 'bailiff' is derived is '*balivus*' which itself came from 'baiulo' – 'to carry a heavy burden', so that a '*balivus*' was originally a 'porter'. Over time, and as the word passed into English, the 'burden' became more figurative and suggestive rather of the 'burdens of office' associated with a bailiff's duties.

The changes in the manner in which the town was administrated would have been occasioned by the increased power in the hands of the burgesses. But the increasing trade and commerce with their consequent population expansion, particularly the transient population such as soldiers, sailors and itinerant tradesmen, generated other social changes, not least of all those connected with law and order.

There was no body of men resembling what we might think of today as a police force. Nor was there anything resembling a modern fire brigade, which, when we think of the tiny wooden houses and shops packed together in a tiny cluster on the banks of the Mersey and all those open fires, must have meant a serious conflagration was an ever-present danger. We can only assume that houses and townsfolk were guarded against fire and theft by a sort of medieval 'neighbourhood watch' system. If a thief was detected he was chased through the streets and justice, if and when he was caught, was probably swift and summary. And if a fire broke out, we can only assume that the people of Liverpool came out *en masse* and stood in lines passing buckets of water hand-to-hand up from the Mersey to wherever the fire happened to be.

The main institution of legal authority was, as we have seen, the Portmoot, and miscreants were kept in check largely through the good offices of the bailiffs. But there was also one other official who tends to be neglected in history books: the scavenger. It was the scavenger's job to make sure that the markets were run in a reasonably efficient manner and that the traders tidied up after themselves at the end of the day, so that at least a modicum of cleanliness could be maintained.

The Scavenger

We now use the term 'to scavenge' in a denigratory way to describe animals or people who rummage through rubbish looking for something to eat. But in the Middle Ages a 'scavager' (the original spelling) was a market official whose principal task was to make sure that foreigners who wished to trade on a town's market had paid the relevant taxes and had permission to display their goods. Later on he assumed the additional responsibility of making sure all the rubbish was cleared away and this is why we now associate the term with discarded detritus*.

* For more details see *Word Routes* by Alexander Tulloch, Peter Owen, 2005

But the commercial and social advances enjoyed by the town in the mid-fourteenth century were dealt a hammer blow which could have proven fatal. England was swept by a dreadful scourge known as the Black Death (technically Bubonic Plague) and hardly a corner of the land was left untouched. Liverpool was no exception and the cramped, unsanitary conditions (effluence was only washed away when it rained) provided precisely the environment needed for the plague to cut through the community like a knife through butter. In 1361 people were dying so fast that the authorities could not keep up with the burials, and transporting the corpses to the parish church at Walton was just not an option. Special permission had to be obtained to use St Nicholas's churchyard, situated almost on the water's edge, as a graveyard.

Hard on the heels of the plague came another upheaval which could have seriously damaged Liverpool's mercantile development but, as we now know, probably helped it. In 1381 the country was gripped by an uprising of the peasantry who suddenly realised that they had an ace card to play. The whole country had been so ravaged by the Black Death and the population reduced to such an extent that the county's workforce was greatly reduced. The peasants suddenly realised that they now had the whip hand when it came to bargaining with their lords and masters. Fields still had to be sown, harvests had to be harvested, trees had to be felled and corn had to be taken away for grinding. But now there were far fewer people to perform all these tasks and so those who were left used their bargaining power and demanded better working conditions and higher wages. In Liverpool the peasants demanded an end to the privileges of the chartered burgesses and, in 1382, Richard II issued another charter abrogating the rights of the burgesses to exclude from trade any persons who were not members of the Merchant Guild of the borough. It was another step in the social development of Liverpool.

Meanwhile, elsewhere . . .

1222	St George's day adopted as a national holiday
1238	Consecration of Peterborough Cathedral
1276	Edward I invades Wales
1290	Jews expelled from England
1332	Parliament divided into House of Lords and House of Commons
1345	Building of York Minster completed
1362	English replaces Norman French as language of parliament and the law courts
1377	Introduction of the Poll Tax
1382	Wyclif condemned for translating the Bible into English

4

PEOPLE & PLACES

We can be forgiven for thinking that history is little more than the study of how people relate to places, but this is frequently the case. Name any site of historical importance or interest and almost immediately people associated with it will spring to mind. Waterloo reminds us of Wellington and Napoleon; Munich makes us think of Hitler and Chamberlain and for any Irishman the mere mention of the Boyne or Drogheda will suffice to recall William of Orange or Oliver Cromwell. By the same token all we have to do is think of some famous historical figure and our mind will make the simultaneous connection with a place. Shakespeare recalls the Globe or Stratford-on-Avon; Henry V conjures up images of Agincourt, and for just about any Englishman the mere mention of Nelson will trigger associations with the Battle of Trafalgar. But to advance a theory of why this should be so is almost to quote the obvious: people of drive and vision influence the course of history. And in the process these movers and shakers leave their mark on their physical environment.

And so it is with Liverpool. What had been nothing more than a tiny village at the beginning of the thirteenth century began to evolve a hundred or so years later as changes occurred and local characters began to emerge and take a leading role in decisions affecting the development and evolution of the town. A fisherman in the thirteenth century, approaching the shore in his tiny fishing smack, would have been greeted by nothing more than a few houses and taverns, probably all single storey and none of which would have stood out as being particularly remarkable or of special note. But his descendent in the mid-fifteenth century would have been met by a very different view. Now these same dwellings would have appeared sandwiched between two looming edifices at each end of the town, the castle and the Tower. At first glance they might have appeared to dominate the town like enormous sentinels guarding the good people within. But they sent out a double message: they were supposed to warn potential invaders that the town was well guarded, but at the same time they reminded the denizens of the town that they were subject to the laws, whims and wishes of the local barons and powerful families who had risen to prominence in the area through wealth, marriage and, in some cases, murder.

The Tower at the junction of what is now Water Street and the Strand. The site is now occupied by an imposing apartment block designated 'Tower Buildings'.

Both the castle and the Tower were associated with some of the main players in the history of Liverpool, starting with King John. It was he who thought it would be a good idea to complete the creation of his new borough with the addition of a fine and imposing castle, but he died before he could turn his dream into reality. It was not until sixteen years after John's death that William de Ferrers cut the first sod and the foundations were laid of what was to be Liverpool Castle when it was finally completed in 1237. And from that date the skyline of Liverpool was changed forever.

And the result was pretty impressive, as far as we can judge from the scant information available to us. No contemporary drawings of the castle survive, but we do know enough from documents of the time to be able to build up a reasonably accurate picture of how this magnificent structure would have appeared to the inhabitants of the town.

For a start there is the position the castle occupied and its sheer size. It was built on the headland overlooking the Mersey but the guards on the ramparts would have had a clear view in any direction. They would have seen out across the river and been able to detect any vessel approaching long before it reached the shore. If they turned 90 degrees to the right they would have had an unobstructed view down modern Castle Street and another 90-degree turn would allow them to see out across the orchards and fields extending into the distance over what is now Lord Street.

The construction seems to have been fairly standard for the time. We cannot be certain about the measurements and there is some difference of opinion among historians, but it seems most likely that the overall shape of the castle can best be described as a distorted square with 5ft-thick ramparts measuring 114ft × 108ft × 105ft × 111ft in length. The north tower housed a gatehouse and barbican overlooking two large courtyards, one of which contained the castle well, protected by a wooden cover and known as the 'house'.

At the base of the south tower there was a little chapel, and the west tower (the largest of the three) housed the Great Hall which would have been used for banqueting on a grand scale.

Artist's impression of what the castle might have looked like in the Middle Ages.

An impression of the castle in 1689

But just how often the Great Hall witnessed banquets for the great and the good is difficult to say. The castle dominated the town for about 500 years, but for much of that time it lay empty, or at the very least, seriously under-used. We know for instance that during the Middle Ages it was presided over by a constable (who also doubled as the Ranger of Toxteth Park and the deer parks at Croxteth and Simonswood) on a salary of £6 13s 4d per annum, but that he did not live in the castle but in a little house just outside the gates. We also know that its military purposes were somewhat limited. No standing garrison was based within its walls and it seems to have been used mainly as a gaol. The only permanent staff on duty here, according to the records, were a watchman and doorkeeper who were each paid the magnificent sum of three halfpence a day, out of which they were expected to buy their own meals.

Constable

This is another word which has changed its meaning almost beyond recognition over the years. Originally it meant no more than the lad who looked after the horses, derived as it is from the Latin word '*comes*', meaning 'attendant' and '*stabulum*', which is our word 'stable'. By the thirteenth century it had moved up the social ladder a bit and designated a governor of a royal castle. The meaning we attach to it today, i.e. an officer of the law, dates from the fourteenth century.

One of the few times that the castle saw what might be described as military action was during the Banastre revolt in 1315. A certain Sir Adam Banastre had something of a disagreement with the King and gathered a group of malcontents and marched against the castle, which at that time was under the control of Earl Thomas of Lancaster. Their attack came to nought as the defenders were able to stave off the onslaught and the mob retreated in short order. For a while Banastre and his supporters continued to cause a few problems for the King, but eventually the rebellion was quashed and the rebels were put to rout at Preston, the Lancashire town situated about thirty miles from Liverpool.

In 1445 Richard Molyneux, a baron who supported Henry V at Agincourt and who could probably trace his family tree back to the Normans who landed with William at Hastings, became Constable of Liverpool Castle and thus began the lengthy association between the Molyneux family and the castle and, later as the Earls of Sefton, an association which continues even today. Prior to this the Molyneux (originally their name was Molline, but for some reason it was changed to Molyneux in the thirteenth century) had occupied the manor at Sefton from about 1100.

Sefton

The part of Liverpool known as Sefton takes its name from the Anglo-Saxon words 'sef', meaning 'sedge', and 'tun', meaning 'farmstead'. Presumably in the dim and distant past there must have been a farmstead in the area close to a river or pond where sedge grew in abundance.

The other building which became part and parcel of the Liverpool landscape was, of course, the Tower, situated right down at the water's edge at the junction of what is now Water Street and the Strand. The Tower itself is now long gone; it was demolished some time around 1820 (estimates among historians differ) although the association still survives in the name of the modern apartment block known as Tower Buildings.

Originally, this had been the townhouse of the Stanley family (the future Earls of Derby), a family which eventually came to equal if not surpass the Molyneux family in terms of power and influence in the area. They had originally been the de Audley family, residing some way away in the county of Staffordshire with their home in the village of Staneleigh. It is not clear exactly why, but at some point during the reign of Henry III they decided to adopt the village name as their family name and this evolved into Stanley.

One member of the family, a certain John Stanley, served with the Black Prince at Poitiers (1356). He was appointed Lord Lieutenant of Ireland by Henry IV and, as a reward for the sterling service he rendered at the Battle of Shrewsbury and the part he played in the defeat of the Percy rebellion, he was granted the Isle of Man (1405) over which his Stanley descendants ruled until 1737. And the only commitment

Stanley had to agree to was to make a gift to the King of two falcons every year on the anniversary of his coronation. A year after being granted what was virtually the kingship of the Isle of Man, John Stanley was also given permission by the King to strengthen his Liverpool townhouse. What this meant in fact was that he was allowed to develop it into a fortified building of such dimensions that it almost rivalled the castle in size. But this was probably the intention. The rivalry between the Molyneux's and the Stanley's reached such a pitch that it eventually went beyond the bounds of straightforward 'one-upmanship' over who had the most prestigious living quarters. In 1425, Richard Molyneux marched a band of his men to the Tower and was ready to do battle with his rival, but it appears from contemporary accounts that no blood was spilt although the rivalry remained and indeed lasted for at least the next few centuries.

If the Molyneux's and Stanley's were the apex of the social structure of medieval Liverpool, just below them in position, wealth and importance were the Lords of the Manor. The town of Liverpool was surrounded by ancient Saxon manors such as Everton, Walton, Childwall, Garston and Fazakerley, all of which are known to today's Liverpudlians (or should that be Liverpolitans?) as suburbs of Liverpool, swallowed up remorselessly by the great conurbation as it spread out from its original few streets. Many of the families occupying these manors were among the first to answer John's call for his people to come and settle and take out burgages on the banks of the Mersey. And as they were already landed gentry, the burgages they acquired would have made them even wealthier and brought them even greater influence and prestige.

This was the stratum of society that provided most of the middle-ranking officials who assumed the responsibility (and not a few of the advantages) of administering the town. It was from their ranks that the mayors and bailiffs were selected and they controlled much of the economic activity of the port. They controlled the land, the fisheries, the ferries and the flourmills and presided over the manorial courts. These were the people who also stipulated how much bread and ale could be sold for and ensured that the bakers and brewers never sold produce which failed to meet their exacting standards.

By the middle of the thirteenth century, two other families in particular had emerged who would play a dominant role in the life of the borough over the next 500 years: the Moores and the Norrises. And even today, although their political and economic power in the town has diminished if not disappeared, their historical presence can still be detected in Liverpool's geography and the family names among the inhabitants. A casual flick through the Liverpool telephone directory reveals dozens of Moores and Norrises, as well as the descendents of old baronial families the Molyneux's and Stanley's.

Both the Moore family and the Norrises may have been scions of old Norman families, but we cannot be certain about this. But we know that in 1246 a certain de Mora (the original spelling of the name) was a reeve in Liverpool and two half-brothers, John and Alan le Norreys (later Norris), acquired a part share each in the old manor at Speke through marriage around the middle of the thirteenth century.

The moat at Speke Hall

Speke

The district of Speke (and the manor associated with it) is thought to derive its name from the Anglo-Saxon word 'spec' meaning 'twigs', 'undergrowth'. If this is the etymology, it is safe to assume that the whole area was at one time covered with particularly dense trees and bushes which had to be cleared before the land could be built on by our Saxon forebears.

History seems to suggest that these two dominant families were alike in some ways but very different in others. They both saw the advantages in terms of wealth and power which could be acquired through the ownership of land and property. The Moores, associated more with the north end of the town, fairly soon acquired lands outside the boundaries of the borough and became lords of the manor in places such as Kirkdale and Bootle. To the south it was the Norrises who acquired the old manor at Speke, but considerably increased their family fortune by adding land in Garston and West Derby to their portfolios.

Bootle

Situated about three miles from the centre of Liverpool, the old village of Bootle grew up around what must have been an estate of some importance in Saxon times. It features in the Domesday Book as Boltelai, but today's spelling is closer to the Anglo-Saxon original, *botl*, which, from the end of the tenth century, designated any dwelling but particularly one such as a manor house with adjacent lands from which the lord would derive a substantial income.

But the manner in which these families operated was very different and their attitudes to the social graces seems to have had very little, if anything, in common. The Norrises included what today would probably be described as some very dodgy characters. In fact, murder seems to have been, if not exactly a family occupation, then at least an activity which did not prevent them sleeping at night. In 1360 and 1352 respectively, John le Norreys and Alan le Norreys were both pardoned for murder. Perhaps more interesting, however, is the leniency with which they were punished: they both had to serve with the King's army, John in Gascony and Alan in Brittany. Another Norreys, Henry (although now the spelling of the name is recorded as Norris) was knighted, despite being a well-known rogue described at the time as a 'malefactor of the forest'. We also know from contemporary records that this same Henry had a bevy of mistresses by whom he fathered more than just a few illegitimate children.

The main entrance to Speke Hall

One of the grand oak-panelled rooms of Speke Hall.

The Moores, on the other hand, seem to have been a more peaceable family altogether. They worked hard in their efforts to build up their estates and much of their income and wealth was derived from milling. In medieval times this was probably one of the most important professions: flour and bread was the staple diet and for many households would have made up a considerable part of the daily food intake. A miller in Liverpool, along with the brewers of beer and ale, would have been assured of a steady income as the economy of the area was still based largely on agriculture. The combination of property ownership and milling gave the Moores a very healthy income.

Of course, we cannot be absolutely sure as to which occupation contributed more to the wealth amassed over the years by the Moore family. All we can be sure of is that they did gain considerable wealth and that they did what most families did (and still do) when they realised how much their coffers had swelled: they moved house. The family moved to Bank Hall in Kirkdale, where they could enjoy the benefits of good clean air and country life away from the increasing noise, filth and general discomfort of a growing town and commercial centre. As a consequence, their 'old hall' became known as 'The Old Hall', a name that survives today in the name of the thoroughfare we know as Old Hall Street.

The Norrises live on in the name they have bequeathed to us in the vast urban sprawl known today as Norris Green. Less obvious, however, is their association with Speke Hall. Situated to the south of the city near to what used to be Speke airport but was re-named John Lennon airport in the 1990s, this beautiful old manor house now sits anachronistically in the middle of a sprawling industrial estate. Visitors to the site travel back in time as they pass the twentieth-century factories and warehouses for a guided tour through the oak-panelled rooms, halls, walkways, bedrooms and kitchens, where they can soak up the atmosphere of a bygone age and attempt to imagine what life must have been like for the rich and powerful all those centuries ago.

The original Speke Hall was an ancient Saxon manor, which, by the fifteenth century, had probably fallen into a state of disrepair. Sir William Norris is thought to have demolished what was left of the old sandstone building and begun a period of rebuilding, alteration and extension which was to continue for the next few centuries.

As far as we can tell, both the Norris and Moore families, notwithstanding the former's more unsavoury members, took their civic responsibilities seriously. Both families were staunch supporters of the Church, and the Moores are thought to have played a not unimportant role in the creation of an educational policy for the youth of the borough. They took charge of the administration of finances which had been set for the establishment of a schoolmaster's post in the town and one such office-holder, Richard Mather, was later to achieve fame as a prominent Puritan, chiefly remembered for the works he wrote and published after crossing the Atlantic and becoming one of the early settlers in America.

Members of the Moore family also served as Justices of the Peace for Lancashire, and one of their number, Edward Moore, was appointed Sheriff of Lancashire in 1620.

Meanwhile, elsewhere . . .

1400   Death of Geoffrey Chaucer
1419   English forces capture Rouen in France
1420   Treaty of Troyes recognises Henry V as heir to the French throne
1431   Joan of Arc burned as a witch at Rouen
1477   Caxton produces the first printed book in England

5

UNDER THE TUDORS

A ll the singing and dancing, the bonfires, feasting and general merriment that greeted the accession of Henry VIII to the throne of England in 1509 probably meant very little to the people of Liverpool. The country as a whole was about to experience changes of seismic intensity but at the end of the fifteenth and beginning of the sixteenth century, Liverpool was on her knees. The burgesses were probably more concerned about the survival of their ravaged community than with events outside the borough. The terrible scourge of the Black Death had reduced her population to such an extent that it only climbed back to a total of approximately 700 by 1565 (the population of England in Tudor times hovered around the three million mark) and it was not until 1590 that it reached 1,000 again. In other words, at the end of the sixteenth century, Liverpool still had fewer inhabitants than it had it 1346.

But recovery did take place. It was very slow at first and was dependent on outside influences for its momentum, but nevertheless, as Henry's grip on the country increased and became more and more autocratic, the changes he introduced permeated the whole land and this included Liverpool. But the changes which occurred at this time were not only due to the gradual osmosis effect which might have been expected to filter through to the town anyway. Henry took a direct interest in Liverpool's affairs for two main reasons. In the first place, he harboured strong suspicions that he was being defrauded of his rightful dues by his north-western subjects. In 1514 he gave instruction to Sir William Molyneux to find out if the burgesses had been defrauding the Crown by allowing non-residents of the town to join the guild. Then, in 1528, William Moor was ordered to set up an enquiry about the salvage from ships wrecked off the Lancashire coast. By law, any such salvage belonged automatically to the King (church congregations saw nothing wrong in those days in ending their prayers on stormy nights with 'God send us a wreck this night') and had obviously noted that the number of wrecks reported did not tally with the increased wealth flowing (or not flowing!) into his coffers. As Henry VIII was virtually bankrupt, he could not afford to be swindled out of what he saw as being rightfully his, and so his attentions focussed on those

Artist's impression of a shipwreck on a stormy night right next to the tower.

who were responsible for the tolls and taxes which should have been heading down to London.

The second reason for Henry's interest in the port was, once again, Ireland. Like his forbears (and not a few of his descendants) he was preoccupied with subjugating his Celtic neighbour across the sea. And again like his forbears (and not a few of his descendants) his only answer to the situation was a military one. So once more Liverpool and Chester were drawn into the conflict and became ports of embarkation for troops with their equipment, weapons, ale, horses, straw etc. as they set sail to plunder the Emerald Isle.

It might seem rather odd, but there was a perhaps unexpected by-product of Henry's war in Ireland: trade. Apparently the two nations, despite the fact that they were at war (or at least one was using its military might in an attempt to subjugate the other) did not regard each other with sufficient hostility for it to affect their mercantile inclinations. Added to this was the burgeoning cotton industry in Lancashire, where the mill owners probably cared less for war than for profit, and so the sixteenth century saw an increase in the amount of yarn imported through Liverpool on its way to the mills around Manchester.

In fact, as the century progressed and trade with the rest of the world increased (wines and iron were imported from Spain and Portugal) Liverpool's links with

Ireland went from strength to strength. Ships now regularly plied the sea between Liverpool and Dublin, Wexford, Drogheda and Carlingford as knives from Sheffield and pewter cups and trenchers from Chester crossed over to Ireland, and yarn, linen, hides (for tanning in Liverpool) sheepskins and tallow made the return journey.

But to say that Liverpool was fast becoming a flourishing trading port is to simplify matters more than just a little. There were complicated procedures to abide by and strict regulations to follow concerning the conduct of trade, and many people had their fingers in the pie when it came to making money. When a trading vessel entered the Mersey it was immediately boarded by the water bailiffs, who would want to know where the ship was from, what the cargo was and its intended destination. They would also demand anchorage and wharfage fees, the only exception being if the vessel belonged to a freeman of the borough.

Then the mayor and the aldermen of the borough would get together and decide if they were going to demand what was known as the 'town's bargain'. If they decided this was what was wanted, they would enter into negotiations with the trader and this process followed a strict pattern. A 'prysor' (assessor) would be dispatched forthwith to inspect the cargo and put a value on it, then an offer would be made to the trader. If he accepted, the cargo was unloaded and weighed (for which yet another fee would have to be paid) and then the customs officials would make their appearance and demand more money in the form of duty payable. The cargo was then transported to a common warehouse and the cost of all this would incur more expense in the shape of haulage fees. So at this point the trader would have already laid out a fair amount of money and his goods would still have only moved from the ship as far as some dark and dingy warehouse. But now, at least, he was free to start selling and, presumably, recoup what he had already spent and make some profit for his labours. But here again there were rules that had to be abided by. First refusal went to the freemen of the borough, who had the right to buy whatever goods they wanted, but at the price fixed by the 'prysor', not the trader.

If, on the other hand, the trader and the mayor could not come to some mutually beneficial arrangement, the former did have the right to sell his goods on his own terms, but only after paying to do so under licence. No burgess was allowed to buy any goods until the licence terms had been agreed. And as far as non-burgesses were concerned the rules were even stricter: a 'foreigner' (i.e. someone from outside the town) was only ever allowed to buy goods second-hand from a burgess. The only exception to this rule applied to trade in sheepskins and yarns; these could be traded directly between non-burgesses as many of them came from Ireland and the surrounding area of Lancashire but conducted their business in the borough of Liverpool. No doubt such a relaxation of the laws was a way of attracting traders from outside the town boundaries who would boost the local economy by spending money in the hostelries, taverns and bakers' shops during their stay.

There were also strict trading rules for what went on within the boundaries of Liverpool itself. Markets and fairs flourished, as they did in the Middle Ages, and it is safe to assume that they expanded in keeping with the borough's greater contact with the outside world. But once again there was no such thing as just leaving the burgesses and traders to get on with the business of buying and selling. No, there were regulations that had to be adhered to if the stallholders wished to be allowed to ply their trade. In the first place, just as the sea-borne traders approaching Liverpool were charged at every stage of the game, so those who approached from the landward side with the same idea had to dig deep into their pockets before they could even think about making a profit. Somewhere close to the beginning of modern Scotland Road toll gates were erected in Tudor times and no trader was allowed in or out of the confines of the borough without first paying the requisite tolls, or 'ingates' and 'outgates', as they were known.

The markets took place every Saturday and were centred on what are now the High Street and Dale Street, and a mere stone's throw away from the tithe barn erected by William Molyneux in 1524, and from which Tithebarn Street takes its name. Unlike markets today where the traders turn up early in the morning, set out their stalls and then start selling as soon as they are ready, in Tudor Liverpool there had to be a little more ceremony attached to the proceedings. The traders would line up with their goods, the Lancashire men along the east side and the Cheshire men along the west. Sacks of corn, barley etc. were strategically placed with their necks wide open so that, as the mayor and his retinue walked around in full regalia, their officers could inspect all the goods as well as the weights and measures. This concern for weights and measurements was an important development, as it was in Tudor England as a whole, that some effort was first made towards their standardisation, and in this respect at least, Liverpool does not appear to have lagged behind the rest of the country.

When the ceremonial formalities were over the market was declared officially open. But once again we see how the burgesses of Liverpool made sure that they benefited most; for the first hour only freemen of the borough could make purchases. When they had had their pick the market was thrown open to everybody else.

It was much the same with the fairs. These were still held once a year, in November, and seem to have been more or less the same in character as the markets, but on a livelier and grander scale. Exactly how the official opening was marked in the early Tudor period we do not know, but we do know of a custom that began around the year 1520. A certain John Cross, a member of one of the oldest Liverpool families, decided to train for the Church and signed over all his property in the borough after being appointed vicar of a church in London. Some of the monies that accrued from this transaction were used to found the city's first grammar school, thought to have been in the grounds of St Nicholas's Church. But another share of this windfall was used to build the borough's first Town Hall, a thatched building at the junction of Water Street and the High Street. And from 1515 the fairs were declared open by hanging the sign of a hand from its roof or on one of its walls.

Considering how strictly markets and fairs were regulated in those days, there is one feature of their organisation which seems difficult, if not impossible, to explain.

These fairs lasted three days and during that time nobody could be arrested for any misdemeanour. So how were the rules imposed and was there not a serious problem with law and order?

The short answer is that we simply do not know either the origin of the custom or how order was maintained. But the whole idea seems an enormous anomaly when we consider how, in Tudor Liverpool as in Tudor England, the ordinary citizen's life was subject to controls which we today would find intolerable. As the Tudor reign progressed and Protestantism took an ever-increasing hold on the country, the authorities (now the Town Council) in Liverpool adopted a more and more Puritan stance in matters both spiritual and temporal. One of the first changes they came up with was to stop people referring to Sunday as Sunday: in future it had to be known as the Sabbath. No doubt they spotted the inconsistency of the holiest day of the week in the Christian calendar taking its name from pagan sun worship. 'Sabbath' had two advantages: it was more redolent of the early Christian Church and at the same time literally meant nothing more in Hebrew than 'rest' or 'day of rest'. And once they had decided how the day of rest was to be known they introduced another bylaw: all alehouses had to close on the Sabbath. Such a move would have been to remind the people of the borough that on the Lord's day they were supposed to be about their devotions, not supping ale, telling bawdy tales and generally enjoying themselves in their local tavern. This was the day of the week when, resting from their toils, they were expected to attend morning service in a chapel or church, which by now would have been stripped bare of all popish, idolatrous adornment, and spend the rest of the day at home reading from the family Bible and devoting time to quiet contemplation.

And there were other restrictions. Not only did the alehouses have to close on the Sabbath, but they could only trade on the other days of the week with the permission of the mayor. And a licence could be revoked if the landlord did not abide by his promise to keep an orderly house. Gambling was strictly forbidden, as it was deemed too much of a temptation which could keep the citizens away from other more useful activities, and apprentices who were caught playing cards could be whipped. And there was a curfew imposed on young unmarried males as well as servants: bachelors were not allowed out of doors after nine o'clock at night and servants were allowed out after eight o'clock only if they were about their master's business.

But at least there was a certain democratic hue to all these regulations. For instance, yet another rule was that the good folk of Liverpool were responsible for the conduct and behaviour of their houseguests. In 1592 (by which time Liverpool was thoroughly Puritan) the town mayor himself was fined for entertaining guests who, for one reason or another, did not attend church on the Sabbath. And even the poor old parson could find himself in trouble if he got on the wrong side of the Town Council. One was removed from his post for no other reason than that he failed to stop dogs wandering in and out of the churchyard. Another was ordered to get his hair cut or pack his bags, and yet another was fined simply because he cut down an old bush in the church grounds without first obtaining permission from the authorities.

The Town Council was not a body to be disobeyed or disregarded. It had been the brainchild of a former mayor, Edward Halsall, in 1580. He had managed to persuade the assembly of burgesses that with a council consisting of twelve aldermen and twenty-four ordinary members the borough could be administered far more efficiently than had hitherto been the case. Once he had persuaded the burgesses that his idea would work, he set about organising things in his own way. First of all he arranged it so that the members of the new council would sit for life and that, as they died, they would be replaced by new blood chosen by the remaining members. In other words, Edward Halsall did himself no favours. He virtually handed over to the new Town Council all the powers he and former mayors had enjoyed. At the dawn of the seventeenth century, the Mayor of Liverpool had become a largely symbolic figurehead and little more than what we would now refer to as a rubber stamp for the Council's decisions.

Curfew

We now tend to think of this word as a military command for keeping people off the streets at night, but the origin of the word tells us that when it was first used it was a 'health and safety' measure. In the days when the only source of heating was an open fire, going to bed at night and leaving a burning log in the grate could have serious consequences. So at some point it was decided that a bell would be rung in the town telling people that it was time to extinguish all household fires. The term for this in Old French was 'couvrer feu', meaning literally 'to cover fire', an expression which was eventually anglicised and shortened to 'curfew'. The French 'feu' was derived from the Latin 'focus', meaning 'hearth', the part of a house which could draw one's gaze or become the 'focus of attention'.

Considering just how puritanical the Elizabethans could be, it comes as a bit of a surprise to see what sort of entertainment was not only allowed but positively encouraged by the Town Council. Bear-baiting, bull-baiting and cock-fighting were officially sanctioned spectator sports in Elizabethan Liverpool and, although there is no direct evidence to support the theory, some historians believe that there was at some point a bullring somewhere just outside the boundaries of the borough. But we have to put these unpleasant pastimes into their historical context. This was an age when beheading was considered an acceptable form of punishment for relatively minor crimes (or for no crime at all: think of Henry VIII and his wives!). It was a time when a citizen could be hanged, drawn and quartered if convicted of treason, or burned at the stake simply because he held the 'wrong' religious beliefs. Even relatively minor infringements of the law incurred unbelievably cruel punishment; vagrants would have an ear lobe pierced with a red-hot poker. And we should remember that, after the Dissolution of the Monasteries, vagabonds became an ever-increasing problem, as the homeless now had nowhere to turn to for food and shelter. The torturers would have been kept very busy with their glowing irons, and so it is small wonder that people did not lose too much sleep over what we would now consider cruelty to animals.

Meanwhile, elsewhere . . .

1492   Columbus discovers America
1516   Sir Thomas More's *Utopia* published
1545   Henry VIII's ship, the *Mary Rose*, sinks off Portsmouth
1588   The Spanish Armada fails in its attempt to invade England
1596   Spenser's *The Faerie Queen* published
1602   First performance of Shakespeare's *Hamlet*

6

THE EARLY STUARTS &
THE CIVIL WAR

I f the events of the sixteenth century can be referred to as seismic then those that affected the England of the first half of the seventeenth century can be described as tidal. The ebb and flow of peace and civil war, monarchy and republicanism, saturnine Puritanism and Royalist flamboyance marked the early sixteen hundreds as a time of endless change almost unmatched at any other period in the country's history. And Liverpool, which had in earlier times remained largely immune to the events and changes in the rest of the land, now became almost a microcosmic mirror image of what was taking place beyond her boundaries. The whole country was to be affected by the fact that Elizabeth I died childless in ways which they could not possibly have foreseen, as religious, social and intellectual change coincided with the country's expansion and greater success as a trading nation.

Elizabeth's death brought to an end the Tudor dynasty and ushered in the Stuarts from north of the border. In April 1603, when James VI of Scotland set off on his long and arduous journey to London to become James I of England he must have been feeling rather pleased with himself. Not only was he travelling south in the sure knowledge that he had made a reasonable fist of governing Scotland, but he knew that news of his accession had been greeted with an almost universal sigh of relief in England. His new subjects saw in him a monarch who was already married with children, and this would reduce the chances of problems over succession when he died. He was also a Protestant. Under Henry VIII and Elizabeth I there had always been the possibility of invasion by Catholic Spain, and although the danger had at least receded if not disappeared with the destruction of the Armada in 1588, no doubt the possibility of a resurgent Catholic threat was still in the back of many people's minds. So, all in all, James must have been in fairly buoyant spirits and feeling confident that being the King of England would be no different from being King of Scotland. Unfortunately, there were huge differences, as he was about to discover.

Stuart or Stewart

It is sometimes assumed, incorrectly, that Stewart is the English spelling and Stuart is the Scottish. In fact Stuart is the French spelling of the name and this should not be surprising when we consider the origin of the House of Stuart. The family originated in Brittany and was brought to Scotland by King David I, who had a liking for almost anything Norman, in the first half of the twelfth century. The family excelled at estate management and served generations of kings of Scotland as high steward, later spelled stewart, hence the origin of the name before it was spelt *à la française*.

The term 'steward' has a particularly interesting etymology. The first element, ste-, is derived from 'stigo', an Anglo-Saxon word which eventually developed into modern English '(pig)sty'. The second element is the Anglo-Saxon 'waerd', 'guardian', so a 'stigo waerd' or 'steward' was originally the man who looked after the pigsty.*

One of the reasons why the honeymoon period between James and England was rather short-lived was his unshakeable belief in the 'divine right of kings'. He was convinced beyond all doubt that he had been placed on the throne of Scotland, and now England, because he had been chosen by God to rule autocratically and that nobody had the right to gainsay him. A century earlier he would have been on solid ground as this is what people genuinely believed. In those days the vast majority of the populace lived out their lives, from the cradle to the grave, in the certain knowledge that God had determined their 'station in life' and that to question this assertion was as close to blasphemy as damn it is to swearing. But this was a new age. This was an age of discovery and exploration, both in the physical world and in the world of ideas and thought. Thinkers were now starting to ask questions where previously such activity had been a dangerous occupation. Institutions such as the Church and politics were now being re-examined, and more and more people were starting to reject the status quo and were becoming less likely to accept what their parents and grandparents had believed. So it was not all that good a time for a monarch to believe in his own divine appointment or that Parliament governed solely on his say so; particularly as Parliament believed that he ruled solely on theirs.

But there were also other reasons why James fell out of favour both with Parliament and the public as a whole. As a keeper of the purse he was pretty disastrous. He had an ever-increasing army and navy to finance, and this, coupled with his own extravagance, meant that the only way he could raise the necessary monies was to raise taxes. In 1634, the King revived the old method of taxation known as 'ship money', but made one or two adjustments which he assumed would bring in even more revenue. Under the old scheme, communities living near the coast

* For more details see *Word Routes* by Alexander Tulloch, published by Peter Owen, 2005.

were expected to either build ships during a national emergency or pay for them to be built. Charles now added his amendments: the whole country, not just the coastal towns and counties, were required to pay the tax which would in future be levied in peacetime and not just when there was a threat of war. The new tax was vehemently and universally opposed, but, despite the protests, the King had his way.

Liverpool, however, refused to pay. Under Charles's taxation plans the borough should have paid a grand total of £15, but the burgesses, egged on by John Moore, a passionate Puritan, refused to pay as a matter of principle. There is probably no financial reason why the borough could not have paid. Like the rest of the country, Liverpool had been enjoying something of an economic boom as trade with countries such as Spain and Portugal and the emerging colonies brought increased wealth to the town. And we can safely assume that, had it not been for John Moore's anti-monarchist stance, Liverpool might have paid up, albeit somewhat grudgingly. After all, the town had benefited considerably from Charles's benevolence. In 1626 he had granted the burgesses a new and very comprehensive charter, which cleared up many of the old vagaries and misunderstandings. It did away with much of the medieval terminology which few could understand or decipher, and in language plain and clear stated that Liverpool henceforth was an 'incorporated borough' and that the burgesses would in future enjoy all the rights included in previous charters, and would additionally enjoy ownership of all common land and wastes.

But the burgesses, during the civil war, sided with the Puritans (Parliamentarians) against the Royalists. As in the rest of the country, the middle-class traders tended to support the Parliamentarians whereas the nobility and peasantry were the King's men. Liverpool in fact became a Puritan enclave surrounded by a Royalist hinterland. Of the Liverpool nobility, only the Moores supported parliament; the Molyneux, the Norrises and, in particular, Lord Derby were all unwavering in their support for the Stuart cause. With the Tower and the castle in Royalist hands there was very little the beleaguered Puritans could do, and as most of the country fell to the Royalist cavalier armies the future looked very bleak indeed for them. By 1643, Charles's army had taken most of the north and west of the country and the Parliamentarians were forced to ask for help from the Scots, promising to establish a Presbyterian church in England in the event of a victory over the staunchly Anglican Charles. The Scots agreed and sent an army down to lend support, but the combined forces of Scots and Royalist English, under the command of Prince Rupert, Charles's nephew, were beaten on Marston Moor in Yorkshire by a Parliamentary force led by a devout Puritan squire-turned-soldier from Huntingdon, Oliver Cromwell.

The ebb and flow of war passed over Liverpool several times. At the outbreak of hostilities it seemed as thought the Royalists were onto a sure thing and they rested somewhat on their laurels. Commanded by Colonel Norris and secure in the knowledge that the Tower and castle were in Royalist hands, they did next to nothing to fortify the borough against assault. Consequently, when the Parliamentary forces, commanded by one Colonel Ashton (or Asshton), did attack they were able to overcome the opposition, even though the fight was prolonged and bloody.

But the fall of Liverpool to the Puritans did not seem to give the Royalists too much of a headache. On the contrary, Prince Rupert is reputed to have referred to the occupied town as 'a crow's nest which a parcel of boys could take', and he opined that he would retake the town as a mere sideshow on his way up to deal with the Scots invading from the north.

He arrived at Liverpool in June, unaware that the garrison had been reinforced by some 400 men from Manchester and that there were ships lying in the Pool ready to do their bit for the Parliamentarian side as and when the need arose. Women and children had been sent away and the men who remained were ready and willing to fight the prince and his troops, and to make sure that if Rupert was victorious than at least his victory would be a pyrrhic one. But the odds were against them. Rupert's artillery, stationed on the hill where Lime Street station now stands, would have been able to pick off targets down in the town almost at will. Whether or not there was a preparatory bombardment we cannot be certain. But we do know that when Rupert sent his infantry in, the men behind the barricades fought like lions and the Royalists were picked off one by one by the Parliamentarian musketeers. When the battle was over, Rupert had lost no fewer than 1,500 men, and he was forced to rethink. Now he brought his artillery into play and bombarded the town for two whole days before sending his foot soldiers in again. But yet again the defenders proved too strong for the attacking army. Rupert paced up and down in his headquarters on Everton Brow as communications from the north left him in no doubt as to the serious situation up there. He had to do something, and so, on or about 13 June, he decided that he would have to mount a nighttime attack. Using subterfuge and cunning, his army made its way through the breaches made by his bombardment in the town's defences near the Old Hall ready to take on the enemy in bitter hand-to-hand fighting. But nearly all the birds had flown. Colonel John Moore had led most of his men away down to the ships at anchor in the Pool and they had slipped away under cover of darkness totally unnoticed not only by Rupert's men but also by the burgesses of Liverpool. It was an act of unbelievable cowardice from which future generations of the Moore family were never able to recover.

But some of the garrison did stand and fight. Royalist attackers and Parliamentary defenders fought at close quarters in an area close to the Town Hall, until, after much blood had been spilled, the defenders of the town were finally forced to surrender. And, if accounts of the time are any way near the truth, what followed brought little glory to the Royalist troops. They may have been the Cavaliers, but there was little that was chivalrous or gentlemanly in their behaviour. Magnanimity in victory was not their watchword: the town was handed over to the troops to plunder at will in return for their courage and fortitude in battle, and their enthusiasm for revenge was boundless. Six months later it was still necessary for the authorities to order every household to provide a man with a spade to help cover up the corpses.

Cavaliers

The followers of Charles I were first referred to as Cavaliers in 1642 by the Parliamentarians, who used the term as one of abuse. The archetypal cavalier wore his hair long, always carried a sword and swaggered his way through life using exaggerated gestures and speech. Prior to this, however, a cavalier was a horseman or knight, known in French as a '*chevalier*', a term derived from the French '*cheval*', meaning 'horse'.

Somewhat surprisingly, however, the French word 'cheval' was derived from the Latin '*caballus*' which meant not just 'a horse' but 'a nag, a lumbering packhorse'. The same word accounts for our term 'chivalry', but a medieval knight's armour was so heavy that our romantic image of him on a dashing white charger is somewhat wide of the mark. In all probability, his mount resembled something more akin to a carthorse.

The fighting had been vicious, little quarter had been given, but the Royalists had won and Rupert rested a while in the castle before setting off to face the enemy, only to be thoroughly routed at Marston Moor. After the defeat he scurried back southwards through Lancashire, bypassing Liverpool, and not stopping till he arrived in Chester. By now the Royalist cause was lost in the north, if not in the whole of England, and Liverpool was almost the only stronghold left in Lancashire that supported the King. But even Liverpool was now on borrowed time.

In the autumn of 1644 it was the Parliamentarians' turn to lay siege to Liverpool. They did not attack, as the rash Prince Rupert had done six months before, but decided to play the waiting game. Lord Derby gathered an army and marched to relieve the borough, but was intercepted and defeated by Parliamentarian forces. Much the same fate was suffered by a force from Shropshire, and then, to crown it all, Colonel John Moore made a dramatic ship-borne reappearance in the Mersey. The King's men were surrounded on all sides and with every day that passed hopes of any rescue receded further and further into the distance.

This more subtle approach to a military problem paid off. Whereas Prince Rupert's tactics of assault and slaughter had brought victory, it was at a heavy cost. The Parliamentarian siege, on the other hand, put an unbearable psychological burden on the defenders of the town. When they realised that they were surrounded on all sides and there was little, if any, possibility of escape, the cracks started to appear. At first, fifty Royalists slipped out one night and were able to make their escape. Then some of the officers also decided to make a run for it, making contact with the enemy and surrendering on the spot. Eventually the whole garrison surrendered; it was a victory for Parliament and humanity. Not a drop of blood was spilt.

To all intents and purposes this meant the end of the war for Liverpool. Although it still dragged on in parts of Lancashire and the rest of England until 1646, Liverpool was little involved. Its burgesses now settled back into a period of calm resignation as they tried to resurrect the trade which had been interrupted during the events of 1643–4.

The war ended with the surrender of the King in 1646 and England was ruled by Cromwell and his New Model Army for the next five years. Generally speaking, this was not a happy time for the country. Yes, the bulk of the fighting was over, but life under Cromwell was hardly a jolly time. He and his killjoy Puritan colleagues did their level best to make everyone's life a misery: they closed the theatres in those towns that had them, prohibited country folk from dancing around the maypole as they deemed the practice pagan, and even went so far as to ban Christmas celebrations. For the Puritans the birth of Christ had to be celebrated with solemn dignity, not with a brief church service and then a day or two of carousing and gluttony. They even, if the legend is right, banned mince pies and plum puddings, as they believed that such delicious tasting concoctions had to be the work of the Devil! Between 1652 and 1660 the Puritans went the whole hog and banned the celebration of Christmas altogether.

For the people of Liverpool the Cromwellian era was a mixed blessing. They profited enormously, once again, because the Lord Protector (the title Cromwell adopted), like those who had ruled the country before him, sent an army to Ireland and used Liverpool as its port of embarkation. They were also rewarded by Cromwell for remaining such staunch supporters during the civil war. He stripped many of the local Royalist manor houses of their woodland in order to provide timber for the rebuilding of Liverpool. It was also during the Commonwealth period that Liverpool became a separate parish, gathering its own tithes, which henceforth would be used for the upkeep of St Nicholas's rather than Walton Church. This was also a time when Lord Molyneux was stripped of virtually all of his feudal powers in the borough, and the privileges the family had enjoyed for centuries were now transferred by parliament to the burgesses of the town.

But these benefits came at a cost. Like the rest of the country, Liverpool found the Commonwealth government stifling and oppressive. Life was hard enough in those days (in addition to all their other woes, the people of Liverpool had had to cope with another outbreak of plague in 1647) and people felt that they deserved their few moments of pleasure and enjoyable relaxation. The Puritan ethic had been well meant as a counterbalance to the excessive extravagances of the ruling classes in previous ages, but the dour suppression of many of the burgesses' liberties represented a step too far. And furthermore, it had probably not gone unnoticed among the populace as a whole that little had been gained by the war: it is probably no exaggeration to say that the main outcome of the war was that England had executed one religious zealot only to replace him with another. Charles was adamant that he ruled by the 'divine right of kings' and Cromwell never doubted that he had been sent by the same God to depose and execute the King. He rejected pleas to spare the King's life by saying that what he had to do was a 'cruel necessity'. Neither, it appears, could entertain the possibility that his religious conviction and fervour just might have clouded his judgement.

By the time of the Restoration of the Monarchy in 1660, the overwhelming majority of the burgesses of Liverpool, along with the rest of the country, welcomed an end to what they had come to regard as tyranny and supported the reinstatement of the Stuarts, in the person of Charles II, even though many of them had originally supported the Parliament–Puritan movement.

Meanwhile, elsewhere . . .

1605	The Gunpowder Plot is foiled
1606	Execution of Guy Fawkes
1611	Authorised King James Bible first published
1615	William Harvey discovers how blood is circulated through the body
1616	William Shakespeare dies
1620	The *Mayflower* sets sail from Plymouth with the Pilgrim Fathers
1631	John Donne, one of the Metaphysical poets, dies
1649	Execution of Charles I
1656	Tea thought to have been introduced to England
1660	Isaac Newton explains the composition of light

7

THE AWAKENING

The middle of the seventeenth century saw a new beginning both for England and for Liverpool. The monarchy had been restored, the harsh reality of Puritan repression had been discarded and people everywhere were looking forward to what they hoped would be a bright future. And why shouldn't they? Liverpool was on the threshold of a new age when the remaining vestiges of feudalism would vanish as the town acquired an ever more outward-looking, vigorous cosmopolitan character. And the changes just over the horizon were about to affect all aspects of her day-to-day life. Her architecture was about to blossom to such an extent that the writer Daniel Defoe (of *Robinson Crusoe* fame) would describe the town as being no less handsome than London itself.

In 1673 Liverpool acquired a splendid new Town Hall with a design to match anything that London had to offer. The ground floor was open to the elements and consisted of a series of arches supporting the banqueting hall and council chambers above. The idea behind the design was that matters of importance to the citizens of Liverpool could be discussed upstairs while equally important matters such as trade and commerce could progress unhindered below.

There was no reason of course why Liverpool should not enjoy the aesthetic benefits of a new town hall; it was the crowning glory to other architectural innovations taking place within the boundaries of the borough at that time. This was the age when new streets such as Fenwick Street (alternatively spelled Phenwyck, and sometime Phoenix), Fenwick Alley, Bridge Alley, Moor Street and, a little later, Hackin's Hey and Lancelot's Hey were added to the original seven streets of the old borough, and the rapidly expanding town deserved a beautiful public building if only to add the finishing touch.

These physical changes took place at more or less the same time as those affecting the old feudal system of land ownership. This was about to be consigned to history once and for all, and the manner in which Liverpool's internal affairs were to be managed would from now on be more in keeping with the developments in the rest of the country.

Hackin's Hey, one of the early additions to the original seven streets. Even today, if you ignore the yellow lines, this side street retains a somewhat 'olde worlde' atmosphere.

Liverpool had been a slumbering giant since it was granted its first charter in 1207. Wars and burgeoning trade with the outside world roused the giant from his sleep on several occasions and under various monarchs throughout the centuries, only to let him fall back into reverie and inactivity when the emergency passed or trade tailed off. But events of the mid-seventeenth century changed all that. As the country as a whole became more and more of a trading nation, so it came to rely with increasing urgency on her north-western port. And this time (apart from a slight doze during the War of American Independence in the eighteenth century) the giant stayed fully awake and never went to sleep again.

It was a on a late summer's day in 1667 that the giant finally awoke. Emerging from his sleep on the banks of the Mersey, he opened one drowsy eye and spotted a tiny ship, *The Antelope*, on the horizon, heading for the port. As the little craft got closer and closer and the sails got bigger and bigger, the giant sat up and began to take notice. He had seen many a ship sail up the river in the past, but knew that there was something special about this one. The cargo *The Antelope* carried was going to keep him busy for centuries to come.

The cargo, of course, was sugar. *The Antelope* had set sail a year before and was now on her return journey from Barbados, laden with the raw material which, once refined, would provide Liverpool with a very considerable income. And when tobacco was subsequently added as another regularly imported cargo, the giant just got richer and richer and fatter and fatter. During his previous periods of wakefulness this commercial activity had been largely confined to the import of wines etc. from France and Spain and various commodities from Ireland. But such a restricted area of trade was now a thing of the past: from the moment *The Antelope* docked, the world was the Liverpool giant's oyster.

But it was not only sugar and tobacco from the New World that gave Liverpool such a boost in the seventeenth century. Several factors coincided which meant that Liverpool as a port suddenly had to cope with an increased volume of trade that might have swamped a lesser town.

To the west, the Americas had suddenly opened up with all their natural riches, and at more or less the same time Lancashire and Manchester to the east had discovered a talent for trade and commerce which would rely greatly on Liverpool to transport their exports all over the world.

But of course the traffic was not all one-way. Just as Liverpool ships now plied the seas and oceans, so ships of all nations became a frequent sight in the Mersey and at anchor in the Pool. French and Spanish merchantmen were frequent visitors (when we were not at war with them!) but now also were ships from Norway, Sweden, Holland, Germany and the Baltic. At the same time trade with Ireland was in no degree diminished; on the contrary, it increased alongside the sugar and tobacco trade from the other side of the Atlantic to such an extent that Chester, Liverpool's old rival, was finally and irretrievably eclipsed.

Scouse

'Scouser', the universal epithet for a native of Liverpool, is derived from the Liverpudlian's reputed predilection for the culinary masterpiece known as 'scouse'. This delicacy originally consisted of meat, some kind of vegetable (usually potato), and ship's biscuit, and is thought to have been introduced to the nation via Liverpool from the Dutch, German and Scandinavian sailors who began to frequent the port from the seventeenth century.

The word 'scouse' is an abbreviation of 'lobscouse', an anglicised form of an old Scandinavian word. Modern Danish and Norwegian still have 'labscovs' and 'lapskaus' respectively for 'beef stew'. And the first syllable of both these words is related to the Modern German 'labbrig' which means 'sloppy' or 'mushy' when applied to food.*

---

* From *Word Routes* by Alexander Tulloch, published by Peter Owen, 2005.

But there were trading benefits which came about by more indirect causal influences. In fact, rarely can circumstances have conspired together to bring so much good fortune to one place as happened in the case of Liverpool in the seventeenth century. In 1665 and then 1666 London suffered dreadfully. In 1665 the town was smitten by the great plague, which ran rife through the closely packed houses and filthy streets. Then came the Great Fire in the following year, which may have served to destroy the vermin and microbes that caused the previous year's plague, but also left many of those who had survived both catastrophes homeless. Some stayed to pick up the pieces and rebuild their lives: others had had enough and wanted a fresh start somewhere as far away from the capital as they could find. And for some that somewhere was Liverpool. Almost certainly one of their number was a merchant by the name of Mr Smith, who in 1668 built the first sugar refinery in the town, thereby starting up an industry which provided employment to Merseysiders until the industry came to an abrupt end in 1981.

Then there were also wars in 1665 and 1666. This time the conflict was with Holland and the London merchants, benefiting greatly from the increasing trade with America, felt that it was just too risky to bring their cargoes anywhere near the English Channel as too many Dutch men-o'-war loitered in its waters with the intent of attacking ships approaching or leaving English ports. Added to this was the enduring problem of the French privateers that patrolled the coastal waters of southern England looking for rich pickings. The only answer, as the merchants saw it, was to land their wares in Liverpool and transport them overland to the capital. Many a ship's cargo was thus saved from the marauding Dutch and French, but, war or no war, Liverpool made hefty profits from wharfage, haulage and other handling charges of one sort or another.

There was another obvious by-product of the expanding trade enjoyed by Liverpool at this time: urban growth. As commercial enterprises flourished and more and more people flooded into the town, there was simply no alternative to urban expansion; the population now had climbed to about 5,000 and was likely to rise even further. The transient population of merchants on their way to and from Ireland, Spain and now America needed more temporary accommodation than the town could comfortably provide. The settled population of shopkeepers, innkeepers, sail makers, candle makers and representatives of all the other ancillary trades needed homes, warehouses and premises for their goods. So expansion was inevitable and the spread of Liverpool outwards from the centre began and has continued ever since.

Among the first people who foresaw the need for more living space was Lord Molyneux. It must have dawned on him that the land between the castle and the Pool would be far more profitable as a public highway than as an orchard. So, in 1672, he cut a swathe straight through the apple trees as far as the Pool and created Lord Molyneux Street. This, of course, survives today as Lord Street, one of the city's main shopping thoroughfares, sweeping down from Castle Street to the old Pool, modern Paradise Street and Whitechapel.

But Lord Molyneux did not have things all his own way as he attempted to put his grand designs into practice. When he had built his new road down to the water's edge, he wanted to build a bridge from the south side of the Pool to the north. At that time travellers wishing to venture beyond the Pool to the barren heathland on the other side had to use the ferry. Lord Molyneux thought a bridge would be better, but others, notably the burgesses and the Town Council, disagreed with him. The land on which he had created a new street was his to do what he liked with, but the burgesses and Council saw the land to the north of the Pool as theirs. This was known as The Waste and had long been considered common land, not still some tract of real estate belonging to the Lord of the Manor.

But Molyneux went ahead with his plans. The bridge was built, tempers flared and eventually the mayor ordered that the bridge be torn down, and all the materials that had been used in its construction were confiscated. What happened next marked the end of feudal land rights assumed by Lords of the Manor in Liverpool.

Because of the rapid increase in Liverpool's population and the changes the town was experiencing as it completed its transformation from a feudal to a bourgeois society, property and land prices rose dramatically. The value of the land on the other side of the Pool shot up, and the Town Council wanted to be sure that if anyone was going to profit from it, it would be they and not some anachronistic local baron. By way of a rather complicated arrangement, the Council allowed Lord Molyneux to rebuild his bridge and agreed to pay him £30 per annum in return for two pence per annum in rent; this was meant to be a token of his recognition that the Council owned The Waste. If this agreement did not signal the final nail in the coffin of the feudal system of land ownership in Liverpool, then it was very close to it. But when Lord Molyneux also agreed to sign over his fee farm lease to the Council for 1,000 years, that was it. The lid was on the coffin and the very last nail had been well and truly hammered down. The political character of Liverpool had changed forever.

Although now stripped of nearly all meaningful authority, Lord Molyneux did still hold the hereditary rank of Constable of the Castle. But, as the fortress had largely fallen into a state of disrepair and there was no garrison there, the power suggested by the title was illusory rather than real. And a few years later Lord Molyneux, being a staunch supporter of James II and implicated in a possible Jacobite rebellion in 1694, was stripped of his constableship, and with it went the last vestige of the power his family had enjoyed for over 200 years.

As the century progressed and Liverpool continued to grow, so did the confidence of its burgesses. There was a new class of citizen making its mark on the political scene and ideas concerning wealth were undergoing a period of re-evaluation. No longer was wealth left in the hands of a favoured few who just happened to be born into the rich, land-owning classes. This was the dawning of the age of the bourgeoisie: merchants and tradesmen could benefit in a way which they had never been able to do before. They could set up businesses and (once the relevant taxes had been paid) they could amass their fortunes as they wished. As the Moore and Molyneux and Norris family stars waned, so those of the new breed of entrepreneurs, the Williamsons, the Claytons, the Tarltons, the Johnsons and the Clevelands waxed. These were the people who now exerted great influence and power, through their commercial skill and *savoir-faire*, over the ordinary people of Liverpool.

As the eighteenth century loomed, Liverpool experienced changes in its social structure, which altered its personality forever. The first of these changes was ecclesiastical in nature. During the Commonwealth, as we have seen, Liverpool became a parish in its own right and no longer a far-flung corner of the parish of Walton. But this arrangement lasted only until the restoration of the monarchy, when many of the old institutions were reinstated and Liverpool was demoted and stripped of its status as an independent parish. But the burgesses, who were now a far more influential body than they had been during the middle years of the century, requested (or even demanded) that they be granted independent parish status again. And they won. At about this time the authorities realised that the old St Nicholas's Church, which had served the population of Liverpool faithfully since soon after the town's creation, was now far too small. As the town had grown so had its population, and it was now felt that a new church was needed to cater for the spiritual needs of the ever-increasing number of citizens. Coincidentally, this realisation dawned not long after Lord Molyneux had built his bridge over the Pool and made The Waste more accessible. So a site was sought for the new church, to be known as St Peter's, and the land chosen was on what had, until very recently, been nothing more than a blasted heath to the north of the Pool. For some strange reason, St Nicholas's and the new St Peter's had equal status, and so Liverpool, in the space of a few years, had gone from having no parish church to having two! History, however, played a trick on the parishioners of Liverpool: the old church of St Nicholas was deemed inadequate for the expanding population of the borough and St Peter's was intended to replace it. But today St Nicholas's still stands in all its glory on the water's edge and St Peter's is no more. The site it occupied until the 1920s is now covered with shops and department stores and its memory survives only in name of the city's main thoroughfare: Church Street.

The second change to overtake Liverpool at this time was political. Just as the rest of the country was evolving new methods of government and witnessing new ideas of social justice and commitment, so Liverpool turned its back on the old systems of administration. A new terminology was entering the world of everyday politics: people were getting away from the habit of categorising individuals and groups according to religious persuasion or which claimant to the throne they supported. The new groupings took shape as a result of the increasingly powerful driving force in society: commerce. Of course the division was not clear-cut, and the new parties, as well as catering for the new breeds of entrepreneurs, contained elements of the old divisions as well. The Whigs and Tories, as these new groups were called, were both Monarchist parties, but the Tories clung to the old idea that the King (or Queen) ruled by divine decree, whereas the Whigs had less outdated ideas on how and why a monarch should rule. For them (as with the earlier Puritans under Cromwell) the king governed only with the consent of 'the people', and 'the people', at least as far as Liverpool was concerned, meant the prominent merchants of the borough such as Thomas Clayton, William Norris and Thomas Johnson.

Whigs and Tories

The strange thing about these emerging new political parties is that they both adopted what had originally been terms of abuse levelled at them by their opponents. The Whigs took their name from the Scottish cattle drovers who, in the minds of the English Royalists, were associated with the Presbyterian Covenanters who wanted to impose their extreme religious beliefs on the country as a whole and not just Scotland. The word 'Whig' is an abbreviated form of 'whiggamer', a combination of 'whig', and old Scots word derived from the Gaelic 'uigean', meaning 'wanderer' or 'fugitive', and the English 'mare', a female horse. The two elements combined meant 'horse rustler'.

The Whigs, not to be outdone when it came to firing off insults, referred to the old Royalists as 'Tories', thereby associating their opponents with Irish noblemen who lived by robbing and terrorising their tenants whilst claiming to support the English throne. The Irish Gaelic word from which the term is derived is 'toiridhe', meaning 'robber' or 'highwayman', and is itself derived from a noun meaning 'chase' or 'pursuit'. In the sixteenth and seventeenth centuries, the term 'toryism' was synonymous with 'banditry' and 'brigandage'.

By 1672, the Tories had achieved a position of dominance on the Liverpool Town Council, but the new boys, the Whigs, dominated the Assembly of Burgesses and the business interests of the borough. This was not a particularly good recipe for peace and harmony, and in Liverpool, again reflecting the situation in the country as a whole, the opposing stances on various issues adopted by the two groups frequently led to bickering, argument and internecine power struggles.

In the struggle for supremacy between the Tory Council and the Whig Assembly of Burgesses, the Tories usually won. Neither group was above a little chicanery and devious manoeuvring in their constant struggles for dominance, but when things looked as if they were going the wrong way for the Tories they employed a tactic which seldom failed. They applied to whoever was on the throne at the time for a new charter, and were almost always successful in their petition. During the reign of Charles II, the Liverpool Tories played the religious card. They appealed to the King for a new charter on the grounds that their loyalty to him was absolute and that, with all the rumours of a Popish plot flying around, he could rely on them for support if and when the Catholics attempted to take over the country. The irony here, of course, was that Charles was a closet Catholic (who, incidentally, converted to Catholicism on his deathbed). But he did not let his religious convictions and sympathies interfere with his pragmatic management of Liverpool politics and politicians. In 1684 Liverpool was required to hand over its old charter to a representative of the Crown (no less a person than Judge Jeffreys, he of the Bloody Assizes fame) at Warrington, and receive a new one. The original petition had been made to Charles, but he died before the new charter was ready, and so when it finally appeared it was signed by the new monarch, King James II.

When the members of the Town Council saw the new charter they were horrified. It still preserved the Tory ascendancy but James had added an additional clause giving the Crown the right to remove or appoint borough officers and members of the Council at any time. Not surprisingly, such a clause had the effect of making the Council members henceforth less than arduous in their support for the King. They felt that he had overstepped the mark and these feelings were compounded not long afterwards because of the Richard Lathom affair. Richard Lathom and his wife were Catholics and lived in the area following innocuous professions (he was a surgeon and his wife a schoolmistress) which, viewed from the standpoint of the twenty-first century, could only be considered as respectable and beneficial to society. But in the latter half of the seventeenth century these occupations were not open to Catholics. The Liverpool Town Council instituted legal proceedings and prosecuted the good doctor and his wife, but when news of the court case reached the King he took steps to defend 'the criminals'. A royal mandate was issued demanding an immediate end to the proceedings and the Deputy Mayor and a senior alderman (both Tories) were removed from office.

To make matters even worse, James began testing the water with members of the Liverpool Council in an attempt to drum up support for those members of Parliament who were trying to have the Test Act of 1673, which banned Catholics and Non-conformists from positions of public office, repealed. Not surprisingly, the Town Councillors in Liverpool saw the way the wind was blowing and with few pangs of conscience switched their allegiance to William of Orange in the lead-up to what is now known as the Glorious Revolution of 1688.

In 1691, William III (William of Orange) granted Liverpool another charter. But this 'new' charter was essentially just a restatement of that which had been granted by Charles II and the James II charter, with its royal prerogative over the hiring and firing of Council members, was quietly forgotten. This new charter had been requested once again by Liverpool Tories as another attempt to have their dominant position not merely confirmed but writ in stone. Unfortunately for the Tories, however, the Whigs enjoyed a large majority among the freemen and simply refused to accept any document which enshrined their permanent exclusion from positions of authority and power. After a great deal of political manoeuvring on the part of the Whigs, and downright chicanery on the part of the Tories, the freemen were able to get a representative into the House of Commons who would make their plight heard. The result was that, in 1695, William granted Liverpool yet another charter, which was to remain on the books until the Municipal Reform Act of 1835. In fact the charter of 1695 was just a restatement of the rights and provisions contained in the charter granted to the borough by Charles I in 1626. But it was worded in such a way that much of it was open to interpretation, although on at least one point it was very clear; it restored to the burgesses the ancient right to elect the bailiffs and mayor, irrespective of the feelings of the Town Council. As the burgesses were mainly Whigs, this new charter gave them the opening they were looking for and they were finally able to seize power. The Tories were not ones to accept defeat gracefully and manoeuvred and intrigued for the next seventy odd years to dislodge their opponents from what they saw as their rightful position of hegemony on the Liverpool Town Council.

So far we have concerned ourselves mainly with the movers and shakers who, either because of their inherited wealth or acquired political power (and frequently a mixture of the two) dominated events and influenced the course of the history of Liverpool. But, getting away from the limelight of the political manoeuvrings for a while, we have to mention another of Liverpool's sons whose contribution to science is often overlooked. His life was cruelly short and nobody who reads of his achievements can fail to wonder what contribution he might have made to scientific knowledge had he been allotted even an average lifespan. Unfortunately, Jeremiah Horrocks died aged just 27, but he achieved more in his twenty-seven years than most of us achieve in a full lifetime.

Horrocks was born in 1617 in Toxteth, which was still a rural village situated outside the boundaries of Liverpool. He read mathematics and astronomy at Cambridge and after graduating in 1635 he returned to Toxteth, where he was able to continue his studies, particularly in astronomy, his life-long passion. At around this time he also studied theology and was eventually appointed curate in the little Lancashire village of Much Hoole, between Liverpool and Preston.

Toxteth

This is just one of the many place names in this part of the country that testify to the presence of the Nordic invaders and influence of their languages on the population. 'Toki' was an Old Danish personal name and 'stöd' or 'stadir' were Old Norse respectively for 'a landing place' and a 'farmstead' and either could have been responsible for the second syllable of original place name, Tokestath. So 'Toxteth' could either have been the place where a certain Toki had a farmstead or where he had his own mooring for his little boat.

The Old Norse 'stöd', 'stadir', the modern English suffix -stead, and the verb 'to stand' are all derived from the Latin 'stare' meaning 'to stand'.

Horrocks studied all the works of the leading astronomers of the day but found at least some of their theories wanting. He designed his own astronomical instruments and one of the conclusions he arrived at with these devices was that the orbit of the moon was elliptical, not circular as had previously been thought.

But it was in 1639 that he made his most important discovery. Other astronomers had discovered that it was possible to predict the position of the planets at certain periods of the year. Kepler had worked out that Venus, in its orbit around the sun, crossed between the sun and earth at certain times, and observers on earth, provided they had the right equipment, could watch its progress as it appeared to move like a little black dot across the sun's surface. Kepler went on to predict that the Transit of Venus, as the phenomenon was termed, occurred every 130 years and that the next one was due to take place in 1761, but Horrocks thought Kepler had got his sums wrong. He calculated that Venus would pass between the earth and the sun at about three o'clock on the afternoon of 24 November 1639. The story goes that, as this date was a Sunday, whilst delivering his morning sermon in the little church of Hoole, he gave the distinct impression that his mind was not on the task in hand. He could hardly contain his excitement and it was obvious to all that three o'clock could not come soon enough for him. And he was not disappointed; at 3.15 p.m. Venus did indeed appear as a tiny black speck making its way across the heavens between the sun and earth. His calculations had been correct.

When he died in 1641, Jeremiah Horrocks had, in just a few years, made such a great contribution to our knowledge of the universe that such eminent men in the field as Sir William Herschel and Sir Isaac Newton freely acknowledged the work done by the impecunious curate from Hoole. Herschel referred to him as 'the pride and boast of British astronomy.'

Meanwhile, elsewhere . . .

1667	Publication of Milton's *Paradise Lost*
1668	John Dryden becomes the Poet Laureate
1669	Sheldonian Theatre built in Oxford
1675	Royal Observatory founded at Greenwich
1681	London street lights lit with oil lamps
1684	John Bunyan publishes *Pilgrim's Progress*
1688	Insurance brokers begin trading in Lloyd's coffee house
1694	Bank of England founded by Scotsman William Paterson
1700	Eddystone Lighthouse completed

8

YET MORE CHANGE

The constant changes which affected Liverpool during the first 400 years or so of its life were brought about by the whims of the land-owning barons, the aspirations of the Town Council and war. But the early 1700s signalled the arrival of the new kids on the block: the engineers. And by the end of the century the transformations these modern magicians were to bring about would make the changes of previous centuries look like mere tinkering at the edges.

The expansion in trade, which sent out such vigorous shoots during the previous century, now burst into bloom in a way which few could have anticipated. Ships were arriving in and setting sail from the port with such regularity and frequency that it was soon realised that the old Pool had quite simply outgrown itself. At a little over 1,000 yards long and not very deep it could no longer cope with the volume of traffic or the increasing draughts of the larger ships now being built. Something had to be done or Liverpool's future as a port was doomed.

It was Thomas Johnson, Member of Parliament for Liverpool from 1701 to 1727, who realised the magnitude of the problem confronting the town, and it was at his instigation that the services of the London-based engineer Thomas Steers were engaged. In 1709, a Parliamentary Act was passed granting the borough permission to construct what would eventually be the first wet dock in the world, but so colossal a task was the undertaking that it was not completed until 1715. Hundreds, if not thousands of men must have toiled from dawn till dusk with little more than glorified buckets and spades to dig and move thousands upon thousands of tons of earth and then erect the floodgates needed to hold back the tide. With the floodgates in place, it was then possible to build the stone wall which was to form the basis of the magnificent end product. After five long years, when periods of nail-biting anxiety must have alternated with optimistic anticipation, Thomas Steers and the now Sir Thomas Johnson (he was knighted in 1708), the merchants who gave their financial backing to the operation and the labourers who slaved to make the dream a reality, could look with pride on what they had created. The dock (200 yards long and 100 yards wide) would provide a safe harbour for the foreseeable future for ships of all nations. But the glorious feat was tempered somewhat by a bitter irony:

in order to create a safe haven for modern ships, the old Pool had been drained and the body of water which had been the reason for the town's creation in the first place became just a memory. It had simply ceased to be and would eventually be buried beneath the thousands of tons of concrete that is today's Paradise Street and Whitechapel.

The wet dock proved to be such a runaway success that the burgesses of Liverpool very soon got carried away by yet another burst of enthusiasm for grand architectural schemes and built a further wet dock as well as an additional dry dock which would cater for ship repairs.

But the building of docks was not the only engineering feat of the eighteenth century. During the late Stuart period, the country as a whole underwent a transformation which simply would not have been possible had it not been for the engineering fraternity. In the seventeenth century the roads were still in a terrible state and travel between the growing towns and cities was an arduous undertaking. But the eighteenth century saw modest beginnings in the nation's attempt at solving the problems caused by poor transportation. As trade expanded, there was an ever-increasing demand for improved means of getting men and materials from one end of the country to the other. At the beginning of the eighteenth century the economy of the whole country depended largely on locally based cottage industries and many people varied their jobs and means of earning a living. A smallholding could be managed by some members of a family while others brought in extra pennies by spinning, glove-making or lace-making. In Liverpool, which we should not forget was still principally an agricultural community, many labourers would have combined working on the land with earning what they could in the town. And this system worked well while most produce was consumed locally; but as the industrial age loomed and the population expanded, it became increasingly expedient to build better roads and, if possible, think up new means of distribution.

In the area surrounding Liverpool, one of the first moves in this direction was taken with the construction of new roads between Liverpool, Warrington and Prescot. It seems a small step to us but in the context of the times such civil engineering projects represented major improvements. It meant that Liverpool was beginning to overcome its geographical isolation from its hinterland and communication with the rest of the country was becoming a matter of much greater ease. In fact, once there was a decent road to Warrington (no more than twenty miles away) it meant that the sugar, cotton and tobacco arriving from the West Indies and America could be delivered to all parts of the country, including London, with far greater ease.

But it was not only the improvement in the road system that was to prove such a boon to trade. The development of, and improvements to, inland navigation at this time proved to be at least as important if not more important than the improvement to the roads. As a direct result of improvements to the inland waterways, coal could be transported far more cheaply from the coalfields of Lancashire to Liverpool. The Irwell, a tributary of the Mersey, was dredged and made navigable to barges transporting goods between Liverpool to Manchester. Then, when the self-taught engineer James Brindley created the first artificial waterway by deepening and diverting the less than voluminous stream known as the Sankey Brook, the age of the canal had arrived. And it is probably no accident that another industry developed apace in Liverpool at the same time: pottery. Islington, Shaw's Brow (now renamed William Brown Street), and Dale Street all boasted thriving potteries and, together with modern Lime Street (originally Lime Kiln Lane) provided Liverpool with an industry that achieved such status and renown that not only did it produce its own fine china but decorated much of the delicate chinaware produced in Staffordshire and sent to Liverpool for the purpose. Cartloads of such fragile artefacts would never have survived the journey over the potholed, un-metalled, bumpy roads and so the canals, with their leisurely but smooth progress, offered the only viable alternative.

Once the engineers had acquired a taste for canal building, and manufacturers, bankers and the government realised the advantages of an efficient canal system, every town suddenly wanted one. By 1772 the Mersey was linked by canal with the Severn; by 1777 it was linked with the Trent and when the Thames linked up with the Trent in 1790 it meant that goods produced in Liverpool could find their way relatively safely and cheaply to Hull, Birmingham, Bristol and London. And also, of course, goods produced in these towns could be distributed throughout the world via Liverpool, which would have made huge profits for handling and ensuring that the goods had a safe and efficient transit through the port. Liverpool's industrial and commercial isolation was well and truly over.

Other manufacturing industries which developed considerably at this time in Liverpool included rope-making, shipbuilding, and the now long forgotten but once active industry of clock-making. All of these would have benefited enormously from the improved communications with the rest of the country. And in fact what happened proved to be something of a virtuous circle: navvies swarmed all over the country, laying roads, digging canals, building bridges so that even more itinerant labourers could find their way with even greater ease around the country obeying the call for more and more labourers to work on more and more canal- and road-building schemes.

With all the engineering projects making trade and industry so much easier for the inhabitants of Liverpool in the eighteenth century, it is reasonable to suppose that the lives of ordinary people would have improved also. The population of the town increased enormously at this time (in 1700 it stood at 5,000, but by 1760 there were 25,000 souls living within its boundaries) and it is tempting to think that most, if not all, enjoyed the fruits of the town's new prosperity. But this is not the case. In fact, quite the opposite is true. The merchants who got fat during the Hanoverian era looked after themselves first and foremost. Then they spent lavishly and set in motion a building programme which would eventually transform the town into one of the most beautiful in England. But the beauty of buildings such as the new Exchange and Town Hall, completed in 1754 to replace the one erected in 1673, were mainly for show. Of course trade deals were clinched within its hallowed walls and Council business was discussed and thrashed out within its chambers, but their ostentatious grandeur suggests that they were not merely meeting-places for businessmen. These were places where the increasingly rich and powerful merchants and politicians could parade in all their finery, contemplating how to swell their coffers even further as they turned a blind eye to the squalid conditions endured by those at the bottom of the social pile. The business plans of the grandees were discussed in conspicuous opulence while the poor starved in their hovels only a few yards away.

The working men who toiled day in, day out; month in, month out to build the sumptuous buildings with their lavish interiors and extravagant façades were never allowed to enjoy them. They were not invited to the soirées, the balls or the gentlemen's card games that took place in the various rooms set aside in, say, the Town Hall, for such events. Once their work was done and they had received their pittance they were expected to scurry back to their miserable, over-crowded homes in dark and filthy alleys. For them entertainment was the cockpit, the tavern or the increasingly prevalent Hogarthian gin palace.

In addition to the filling in of the Pool and construction of the new Town Hall, it was the fate of the castle that probably completed the transformation of old, medieval Liverpool. In 1704 the borough was granted permission from the Crown to demolish the castle, the ancient symbol of baronial power, but the former constable, Lord Molyneux, was not happy and he continued to raise objection after objection in a monumental exercise of prevarication and obfuscation. Ten years after the original permission was granted, an Act of Parliament was passed giving permission for a new church to be built on the castle site, but there were so many objections raised in various quarters that another long delay ensued and it was not until 1725 that the castle was finally razed to the ground. Part of the land was now used for the building of a fish market and part, as originally intended, for the erection of a new church in 1726, to be known as St George's and occupying the site where the Victoria Monument now stands. In 1748 St Thomas's was built on Park Lane and this was followed by St Paul's near Old Hall Street in 1769. A few years later, in 1773, St Anne's appeared on Great Richmond Street, and the last to be built in eighteenth-century Liverpool, St James's on Parliament Street, was built in 1774.

The upper echelon of Liverpool society, as elsewhere, strove with ever-greater zeal to insulate itself against the flea-ridden masses. Many of the Georgian houses and squares situated in what, in the eighteenth century, were the outskirts of the town, provided an elegance of lifestyle beyond the wildest imaginings of the town's toilers and grafters. While the wealthy dined and entertained royally in their beautifully appointed homes in the newly-built Rodney Street (laid out 1783–4) or one of the new and spacious Georgian squares, the lives of the socially ignored or forgotten was somewhat different. Not for them the delight of looking out from a tastefully furnished drawing room onto the high hedgerows festooned with honeysuckle and wild roses in the lanes behind Rodney Street. Nor could they have either the time or

This is what Copperas Hill looked like in the eighteenth century.

the inclination to savour the sylvan pleasures of the green pastures close to Lime Kiln Lane (renamed Lime Street in 1790) where cows grazed lazily on the green sward and daisies. And they certainly would not have been welcome among the ladies and gentlemen strolling around the bowling greens on Mount Pleasant or through Ranelagh Gardens, now buried beneath the bricks and mortar of the Adelphi Hotel. For the people of quality these were places where they could relax and listen to an orchestra on a pleasant summer evening or watch a firework display as the autumnal evenings began to cast their shadows. By contrast, the less fortunate languished in cellars and garrets and earned wages so low that the vast majority of them would have had no option but to beg, steal or borrow just to keep body and soul together from one day to the next. We know from records at the time, for instance, that in 1789–90 no fewer than 6,780 people (just over 12 per cent of the population) lived in a total of 1,728 cellars in the borough, without heating or any of the other mod-cons we would now take for granted. Most of these cellar dwellings consisted of just one room, accessed from outside steps leading down from the pavement. Amazingly, there were still people living in these miserable cellars as late as the First World War.

These were the days also when the children of the poor were sewn into their clothing for no other reason than that there were no washing facilities and so there would be no need to take them off and risk getting cold. The alleys and cramped warren-style streets inhabited by the destitute were vermin-infested areas without sanitation, running water or even just plain clean air. So prevalent was vermin that, even as late as the middle of the century, London employed 'rat-catchers royal' and

Copperas Hill today, to the left of the Adelphi Hotel.

'flea-catchers royal' in vain attempts to keep discomfort and disease at bay. There is no reason to suppose that Liverpool would not have employed similar public servants.

And yet there does seem to have been a glimmer of a social conscience that began to make some of Liverpool's sons and daughters feel a little uncomfortable. The intellectual life of the borough was not particularly active in the first half of the eighteenth century; in fact it would be only a very slight exaggeration to say that it was non-existent. In addition to John Crosse's old grammar school, there was just a handful of institutions of indifferent quality masquerading as schools within the borough. There was no newspaper (the *Liverpool Courant* began as a fortnightly publication in 1712 but closed after a couple of months through lack of support), no public library and a university was not even a twinkle in a town planner's eye.

But then things started to change and slight improvements began to be felt in both the education and welfare of the residents of the borough. In 1759 a theatre (built by the same Thomas Steers who built the dock) was opened on Drury Lane, just over the road from the old Tower, and in the same year a private collection of books found a home in a room in a house in North John Street. A gentlemen could pay a subscription of 5s per year for access to the books which he could take home and read by candlelight on dark winter nights, perhaps sitting on a recently purchased Chippendale chair in front of a newly-acquired Adams fireplace with a roaring fire in the grate, no doubt with a glass of something warming at his elbow. This facility may not seem to us to be an event of great importance, but for the eighteenth century it represented a huge step forward in the cultural life of the town. The box of old books eventually grew into the Lyceum Library, housed in a splendid example of Classical Greek architecture which still stands proudly at the bottom of Bold Street. Sadly, however, the building has lost much of its romance and now functions partly as a bank and partly as a trendy bar and restaurant.

The Lyceum was begun in 1800 and completed in 1802. It was, and still is, one of the finest and most beautiful buildings in Liverpool, with a façade consisting of four demi-columns with pedimented windows on either side. Above the central windows are reliefs depicting scenes from Greek history and mythology. On the left is a geographer (possibly Eratosthenes) holding a pair of compasses and apparently measuring the distance between two points on the earth. In the centre is Apollo, the Greek God of agriculture, playing the lyre which, according to mythology, was given to him by Hermes, the Greek God of Commerce and depicted here on the right. Presumably, Thomas Harrison, who designed the building, intended these images as a symbolic representation of those activities which had made Liverpool what it was: world exploration, business and agriculture. And only a downright cynic would point out that Hermes, in addition to being the Greek God of Commerce, was also the protector of gamblers, liars and thieves!

The Lyceum building at the foot of Bold Street. It is one of the most beautiful buildings in Liverpool and yet, in the 1970s, there were people in the city who wanted to destroy it.

Alarmingly, this beautiful example of the Ionic style of Classical Greek architecture was almost lost to us. In the 1970s, during Liverpool's great post-war re-vamp, there were some in the city who thought it was time to demolish the noble edifice and replace it with a shopping centre! Only the dogged determination of conservationists not to see such an architectural jewel destroyed saved it for posterity. The descent from Apollo to Mammon was halted and, for once, commonsense and finer artistic feelings prevailed over what would have been an unspeakable act of commercial vandalism.

The Lyceum

This imposing building at the foot of Bold Street in Liverpool is named after a garden in ancient Athens where the philosopher Aristotle (384–322 BC) taught. The word 'Lyceum' is the Latin form of the Greek 'lukeion', an adjective formed from the noun 'lukos' meaning 'wolf'. This rather surprising association came about from the fact that the garden in question was close to the temple of Apollo, referred to in Greek as 'Apollon lukeios' ('Apollo the wolf-like' or 'Apollo of the wolves') because he was associated with the early dawn, and the greyish colour of the sky at that time of day reminded the ancient Greeks of a wolf's coat. No doubt the architect of the Liverpool Lyceum intended the building to resemble the Temple of Apollo in Athens.*

An interesting feature of the social development of welfare institutions in Liverpool, as indeed throughout the country, is that much of the initiative for social improvement was instigated by individuals, not government. In the eighteenth century, the landed Tories were too concerned with building their grand houses and estates outside the towns to be concerned with either the urban or rural poor. The Whigs, with their roots in trade and commerce, were equally as concerned with building their imposing townhouses not too far distant from their offices and factories, but they too avoided the poor like the plague. In Liverpool, the Whigs, still the dominant political party for much of the eighteenth century, paid little attention to the urban deprivation that surrounded them. Additionally, there was a belief current at the time that to offer the poor more than the absolute minimum of assistance was unhelpful all round. It was costly to those proffering the help and it discouraged the poor from helping themselves. Such ideas were not all that different from those advanced towards the end of the century by Thomas Malthus, who argued that giving handouts to the down-and-outs robbed them of any motivation they might otherwise have had to drag themselves out of the gutter and to make something of themselves. Such high-minded justification for turning a blind eye to the destitute played right into the hands of those who were reluctant to help anyway.

---

* See *Word Routes* by Alexander Tulloch, Peter Owen, 2005

So improvements in welfare, education and health often relied on the good offices and social consciences of private individuals who were perturbed by the misery they witnessed among their fellow citizens. One such benefactor in Liverpool was an old seadog named Bryan Blundell (1674–1756), whose family had lived in Liverpool since Elizabethan times. He teamed up with a certain Revd Mr Stythe, who was also concerned about the brutish lives led by most of the children of Liverpool. In 1708 the seafarer and the vicar bought a small building in the town for the princely sum of £35, hired a schoolmaster for £75 per annum and opened a school for about fifty destitute boys. Almost immediately they started making plans for a grander institution and the result was the Bluecoat School, a magnificent example of Queen Anne architecture which still stands today on its original site in School Lane behind modern Church Street. When his colleague the Revd Mr Stythe died in 1713, Blundell abandoned seafaring to devote the rest of his life and most of his energy, not to mention a tenth of his income, to the school which he had created. On his death in 1756, the number of boys being educated within this oasis of academe had risen to 100. And they all wore the uniform blue coat, which gave the institution its name.

Then there was the question of the sick. As in the rest of the country the prevailing attitude to the halt and the lame in Liverpool was pretty insensitive. If you were ill you did what you could to get better or consulted a doctor, who in most cases could only cure illnesses which would cure themselves anyway without his intervention. In cases of genuine infection and serious illness the only answer Liverpool had was The Waste. There was no cure for the vast array of infectious diseases that ran like wildfire through the population at various times of the year, and the only solution was to isolate the victims on the heathland outside the city boundaries. But by the eighteenth century this was becoming an increasingly less viable option. New building schemes were gobbling up the land beyond the old Pool at an ever-increasing rate, and the population was growing far too fast for the old policy of isolation to be effective; by the time people were diagnosed with whatever ailment afflicted them, the virus had passed on to dozens more who, unknowingly, were passing it on to friends, relatives and strangers alike. So the only answer was the workhouse (one of which stood in Hanover Street from 1732 to 1795 and was ironically also referred to as a 'house of industry'), where patients worked while they were still able and then either recovered and left or took to their beds and died. And this was the system for dealing with the infirm until 1745, when the Liverpool Council took the first tentative steps towards the creation of a public health programme by allowing an infirmary to be built at what were then the outer limits of the town. The first patient was admitted in 1749 to the brand new, purpose-built brick hospital on the site now occupied by St George's Hall.

But care for the less fortunate in society did not stop there. As with the innovative engineering projects of the day, once the idea of caring for the sick became fashionable, more and more charitable institutions began springing up all over Liverpool. Right next to the new infirmary, in 1752, a second hospital was erected, this time for seamen and, in the event of their perishing at sea, for their widows and children. Every sailor connected with the port was obliged to contribute six pence a month for its upkeep.

North John Street became the home of a dispensary in 1778. This was similar to what we would think of today as an outpatients' department at a hospital, catering as it did for the walking wounded rather than the seriously ill. It dispensed medicine and medical advice and was supported by contributions, although, unlike the seamen's hospital, the contributions were voluntary. But unfortunately the contributions seem not to have been all that forthcoming and the dispensary ran into financial trouble. In 1802 it was closed and the apothecary who had been dispensing the medicaments and advice was transferred to the workhouse at a very considerable saving to the parish.

Yet another charitable development at this time was the School for the Blind, opened in 1791 by Edward Rushton, on Commutation Row. Edward Rushton was a blind poet who felt the urge to help those unfortunates who suffered the dual handicap of being both blind and poor. He reasoned that if he could take such hopeless cases and give them some sort of education or trade he would be doing some good in this world, and in this he achieved some degree of success. His pupils were taught how to sing and to play the organ and at least some of them must have reached a fair degree of proficiency as it was soon felt that a new school was needed. A mere nine years after the doors first opened on what could only be described as a risky experiment, the new school was built on London Road. This was subsequently incorporated by an Act of Parliament in 1829 and such was its success that it moved to larger premises in Hardman Street in 1851.

So, all in all, the eighteenth century was a busy one for Liverpool. It saw monumental changes to its geography, its institutions, its way of life and its capacity for commerce and trade of all descriptions. Most of the changes the town experienced can, with justification, be called progress towards a more civilized, caring society. But there was one enormous blot on the sociological landscape: slavery, the subject of the next chapter.

Meanwhile, elsewhere . . .

1706	Creation of the first insurance company
1707	Act of Union binds Scotland and England together as the United Kingdom
1708	Whig government established
1709	Richard Steele launches *The Tatler*
1711	Richard Steele and Joseph Adison launch *The Spectator*
1711	St Paul's Cathedral completed in London
1720	'South Sea Bubble' swindle exposed
1739	John Wesley founded the Methodist Society
1744	First cotton factory in England
1749	Henry Fielding's *Tom Jones* published

9

AN IGNOBLE TRADE

iverpool did not invent the African slave trade. The Portuguese and Spanish had been shipping slaves from Africa to their American possessions since the fifteenth century and were leaders in the field well before England got involved in the eighteenth. Then, when the British did pass laws in Parliament sanctioning the shameful business, the principal ports used by the slave traders were London and Bristol. In other words, Liverpool was very much a latecomer to slavery, but once its commercial genius had been awakened to the fortunes just there for the taking all along the shores of west Africa, there was no holding back. For approximately the last seventy years of the eighteenth century, Liverpool entered into the spirit of the trade with verve and gusto probably unparalleled in all its previous commercial history. In recent years, however, Liverpool, along with the rest of the country, has hung its head and apologised for the part its traders had played in enslaving thousands of Africans. And so it should: the port grew rich and fat on the misery it inflicted on its fellow human beings, just because they were black.

One of the striking features of the history of the slave trade is the extent to which some reverend gentlemen not only accepted the situation but actually attempted to justify it. With unbelievable hypocrisy and cynicism, the Church of England owned and ran plantations in the colonies and profited enormously from the dawn-till-dusk labour of the slaves picking cotton and harvesting sugarcane for their white masters. Some clergymen even claimed that slavery was God's will and quoted passages from the Bible, which, they claimed, proved that the iniquitous commerce was all part of God's plan and that those who argued against it were arguing against His will. When some people of conscience began to voice their doubts about the morality of slavery, and an embryonic abolitionist movement began to stir, a certain Revd Raymond Harris, who in a previous incarnation had been a Spanish Jesuit priest, reached for his Bible. Then, using it like a blunderbuss, he blasted those who dared to suggest that there was anything un-Christian about enslaving one's fellow men. And even more alarmingly, he received a grant of £100 from the Liverpool Council to help him with the cost of producing a pamphlet justifying the slave trade. This pamphlet was published in March of 1788 and contained spurious arguments based on biblical characters and events. His first point, for example, was that Hagar, the slave of Abraham's wife, Sarah, was rebuked by God himself for deserting her mistress. She had been treated cruelly by her mistress but this, according to Harris's interpretation of the texts, made no difference. God ordered her to return and humble herself and beg her mistress for forgiveness. A further example was that of the Gibeonites, who, according to the Bible, had been condemned to serve as the Israelites' hewers of wood and drawers of water till the end of time.

These were just a couple of examples which the ex-Jesuit from Seville cherry-picked for his diatribe against the abolitionist movement. And, just to round things off, he claimed that anyone who did not believe what he said or attempted to refute his arguments could not claim to accept the Bible as the word of God.

Another gentleman of the cloth who saw little contradiction in being a devout Christian at the same time as earning a living as a slave trader was John Newton. He had been born into a respectable household but turned out to be something of a prodigal son. At an early age he ran away to sea and got involved in all sorts of scrapes and dangerous adventures, no doubt mixing with some pretty unsavoury characters on the way. He even, for his sins, ended up a slave in all but name in Sierra Leone, where he was brutally treated and only escaped after some considerable time. To cut a long story short, after his escape he eventually made his way back to England and to Liverpool where he was taken on as a mate on a slaving ship. He proved to be so good at his job that he was soon able to work his way up the promotional ladder to the rank of captain.

Sometime after this he had what must have been a Damascus moment. He saw the error of his previous ways and converted to Christianity. But this devout Christian saw no conflict between his religious convictions and his involvement in the slave trade. Certainly, if the reports about his conduct are true, he treated his human cargo in a far more humane manner than most slave ship captains did. The crew of his 'blackbirder', as the slave ships were known, was not allowed to whip or ill-treat the future slaves of white colonialists; no booze was allowed on board and every day Captain Newton would pray and teach his 'passengers' to sing hymns. For six years, from 1748 to 1754, he plied the high seas picking up his proud Africans around the Bight of Bonny, to the south of modern Nigeria and Old Calabar, and deposited them into humiliating captivity in the Bahamas or Virginia without considering the immorality or injustice of his commerce. He had treated his cargo well; he had delivered men, women and children into a life of servitude, but at the same time he praised the Lord and so his conscience was clear.

In 1754 Newton left the sea and, on his return to Liverpool, began studying the Bible, as well as Greek and Hebrew, with the intention of becoming a Minister of the Church. It was not an easy road for him to travel as there were some in positions of authority in the Church who did not think that 'former captain of a slave ship' would look all that impressive on a parson's curriculum vitae. But John Newton was not easily discouraged and he finally became a minister and, seeing the light at last, took up the cause of the abolitionists. It was at about this time also that he took to writing hymns and so we are left with what some might interpret as a rather embarrassing incongruity. How many people in churches throughout the country on Sunday mornings, giving full voice to old favourites such as 'How sweet the name of Jesus sounds and 'Amazing Grace', realise that they were penned by a man who had sold souls into slavery for a living?

The 'African Trade', as it was euphemistically referred to, was dominated by Bristol from the 1720s to the 1740s, but then Liverpool began to supplant its rival and the reason for this was mainly economic. The plain fact was that Bristol was more expensive as a port and Liverpool took advantage of its cheaper labour costs and geographical position.

Basically, the operation worked as follows: ships would leave Liverpool laden with alcohol, tobacco, cloth, muskets and a variety of assorted cheap trinkets, all of which would be transported to the west coast of Africa. Here they would be

A slave trader with his captive slaves, somewhere on the African coast, awaiting transportation to the Americas.

unloaded and sold to local tribal chiefs who were willing to trade the baubles for their fellow tribesmen. These were then herded like cattle onto unsanitary slave ships and transported across the ocean to the West Indies and the plantations of Virginia, where they would be sold into slavery. The ships' masters would then pick up cargoes of rum, tobacco and sugar and bring them back to Liverpool. The whole round trip would have taken about a year, but the captains, ship owners and probably even the ordinary 'tars' thought it was well worth it: the profits were absolutely enormous. The fact that the men, women and children who were torn kicking and screaming from their native villages never saw their homes again meant absolutely nothing to their captors. And the hundreds who never reached their destination would have been of little or no concern to the slave traders as they counted out their handsome profits once back in their home port. Their purses were fit to burst and that was all that mattered; the Africans who died and were fed to the sharks en route were of no consequence. On the contrary, many of the sick were thrown overboard even before they died and their loss was simply written off as an insurance claim at the end of the voyage.

The conditions endured by the captive Africans on board ship were dire in the extreme. Once they had been torn from their villages, the future slaves were branded with red-hot irons then packed like sardines onto the ships where they had to lie on pallets below decks in stifling conditions for the entire two-month journey across the Atlantic to the Americas. Men, women and children spent almost twenty-four hours a day cooped up in these dreadful conditions. Apart from a brief period of exercise each day, they had to lie there, scarcely able to breathe. As one observer of the time pointed out, they would have had more space to move in a coffin. And if this agony were not enough, there were no toilet facilities. Defecation and urination had to take place *in situ* and if any of the 'passengers' were seasick, their vomit would simply be added to the other bodily effluent. It does not take a great effort of the imagination to visualise the degrading and inhuman conditions these poor people had to endure. Small wonder they had to be chained to each other and to the deck during exercise; more than just a few decided that jumping overboard was a preferable fate.

Those who reached the shores of the New World had no idea what was in store for them. They did not know that the fittest among them had already been sold in advance by private arrangements between a plantation owner and an agent in, perhaps, Jamaica. Nor did they have any idea what was happening when they saw the little boats coming out from the shore, but they must have suspected that their immediate future was going to be no better than their recent past. Then, once the little craft were alongside and strange-looking white men in strange-looking clothes scrambled aboard, grabbing hold of the likeliest looking slaves and tying cords around their bodies to signal ownership, the Africans would have been terrified out of their ebony skins.

The third possibility was that they could be auctioned off. This method, however, was usually reserved for the weaker slaves who looked as though they were too frail to do a decent day's work or so undernourished that they could die at any moment.

These slaves were sold for a song. But even here the commercial sense of the plantation owners came into play. It was not unknown for weak and sickly Africans to be bought for next to nothing and then fed and fattened up till they were restored to health so that they could be put to work. It was a gamble, but if the gamble paid off the owners would have made something of a killing; they had acquired a healthy slave for a knockdown price. But any slaves who looked so puny or ill that they could not even be given away were simply set adrift to die. It was a brutal business.

John Newton came to see the error of his ways, but the same cannot be said of another ship's captain whose name is linked forever with the Liverpool slave trade: Hugh Crow. Crow was born in Ramsay on the Isle of Man in 1765, into a family of meagre means, and went to sea at an early age, losing an eye at some point and thus earning the nickname 'Mind-your-eye-Crow'. But his entrance onto the slave trading scene came rather late in the day and he made his first voyage to Africa in 1790. Once he realised that there was money to be made from slavery he threw himself into the trade with a will. And his determination to succeed paid off; by the time he died in 1829 he was widely renowned as an exceedingly competent captain as well as a shrewd businessman. Unlike Newton, and one or two others who eventually turned their backs on their former occupation, Hugh Crow never changed his mind. He gave short shrift to the abolitionists who were waiting in the wings, even though, if contemporary accounts are to be believed, he treated his cargo so well that, if they chanced to see him after they had settled in America, they would greet him with a genuine smile and offer him a warm welcome.

His conviction that his was an honourable occupation made him hold out till the end, and it was his dubious honour to captain the very last of the slave ships (the Mary) as it made its final shameful trip across the Atlantic before the slave trade was finally abolished on 1 May 1807.

It used to be a commonly held belief that African slaves were brought to Liverpool and put up for sale near the docks on a large square known as the Goree Piazza (destroyed during the Blitz). Schoolchildren of the pre-war years were told that the iron rings fixed into the walls surrounding the piazza were originally where the slaves were manacled and chained, in the freezing cold of this strange Nordic clime, as they waited to be sold and carted off to rich merchants' houses in Liverpool, or more distant towns such as Manchester and Birmingham. But this is not true. What the true purpose of the iron rings was nobody seems to know; they might have been some sort of mooring device for boats and ships, or even just for tying horses to. The only thing we can be sure of is that they were not for restraining slaves. No more than a handful of slaves were sold on English soil, despite the historians' delight in displaying advertisements from contemporary newspapers announcing the time and date of slave auctions. The odd advertisement did appear in the local press, but these were very much the exception rather than the rule. In fact, there was a law in England which stated quite clearly than slavery was illegal in this country and that any escaping slave became a free man the moment he set foot on English soil. This of course is a very laudable sentiment and a noble attitude; what a pity over half a century had to pass before such high-minded morality was applied to those who traded in slaves! It is true, however, that a few well-to-do ladies and gentlemen retained Negro servants, but they were never referred to as slaves. They were employed as personal servants, probably on more or less the same terms as any household maid or manservant in a rich man's home in the eighteenth century.

It is a pity, also, that the lawyers who were so adamant that slavery did not exist in England did not take a stroll along one or two Liverpool streets and glance into some of the shop windows. Had they done so they would have seen the manacles, chains and other instruments of restraint and torture on sale and intended to make life easier for the slave traders who not infrequently had to deal with troublesome, restive captives. One such instrument tells a grim tale all by itself. Many a slave must have hoped to die and find blessed relief from his sufferings by refusing to eat since a device commonly on sale was a steel contraption for forcing an African's mouth open and holding his tongue down. No doubt this cruel piece of contemporary technology was designed to allow the crew, on the orders of the captain, to pour gruel or watery soup down the poor African's gullet. If force-feeding prevented a slave from cheating his owner out of his 'investment', then so be it.

The conditions endured by the slaves in transit and the treatment meted out to them by many of the ships' captains, blinded to the sufferings they were inflicting by the dreams of riches to come, seem inhumane and almost beyond belief to us now. And there can be no justification whatever for even attempting to excuse such behaviour, but we should perhaps try to view it within the context of the times. These were the days when men and young boys slaved down the mines in conditions not much better than those experienced by the Negroes in transit across the Atlantic. These were days when boys as young as 8 or 9 were forced to sweep chimneys by climbing up inside them, or slave from dawn till dusk in the fields or in the houses of the great. Life was harsh for virtually the whole population; creeping industrialisation demanded that men, women and children toil for twelve or fourteen hours a day in stifling, dangerous and deafeningly noisy factories. Unguarded machinery exacted a terrible harvest of severed limbs, and the greatest number of mutilations and serious injuries was found among young children. It was they who were expected to crawl into crevices too small for an adult to squeeze into and then attempt to unravel tangled yarn, free jammed cogwheels or repair broken threads. Finally, at the end of a back-breaking day, men, women and children would return, exhausted beyond a modern worker's understanding, to their pitiful hovels, eat a meagre meal and collapse into bed for some scanty rest before starting the whole process over again the following morning. This, too, was slavery; slavery to machines and to the fire-breathing factories that were springing up all over England's green and pleasant land. Like giant monsters they sucked the workforce in every morning and regurgitated them again at night, day after day, month after month, year after year. Many people either submitted to the demands of the factory owners or they starved. Robert Owen, renowned in school history books as the man whose benevolence gave us the Co-op, employed a workforce of whom, in 1793, twenty per cent were under the age of 9! So it is small wonder that any mention of what the 'passengers' on the slave ships had to endure would have cut little ice with those who could find the time to even listen.

And, away from the land-based factories, many a sailor would almost certainly protest that he had to contend with conditions which were only marginally better than those of the Negro passengers crossing the ocean. After all, this was the age of the pressgang, a legally permitted and government sanctioned way of manning not just a few of the ships that left Liverpool and other English ports to sail away on voyages which would last for months, if not years. The Africans were torn from their loved ones and families never to return, but the same fate could befall a healthy-looking Englishman if he strayed too close to docks. In such places he too could be kidnapped, bundled onto a ship about to leave port, and never heard from again.

But there were some men of conscience who saw the slave trade for what it was: an unjustifiable manipulation of man's capacity for inhumanity.

From the 1780s, murmurings of disgust at the trade began to make themselves heard until those who opposed the trade came together in 1787 and formed the Society for the Abolition of the African Slave Trade. As the movement picked up momentum, several Liverpool-based abolitionists came to the fore as they devoted their energies to ridding the world of what more and more people came to regard as an abomination.

James Currie was a Scot who had travelled down to Liverpool and had opened a doctor's practice in the town. He is mainly known for the tireless way in which he campaigned for better housing for ordinary people, focussing his attention particularly on the filthy and unsanitary courts (tiny, back-to-back housing built around a central yard) where people were expected to live and bring up their families. Currie's genuine concern for the health and welfare of society's underdogs led him to take a natural interest in the poor souls who were enslaved by the merchants and businessmen of his adopted home town.

Edward Rushton, the blind poet whom we have already met as the founder of the school for the blind, wrote *West Indian Eclogues*, a selection of poems in which he pleaded eloquently for freedom and roundly condemned slavery. And William Rathbone (the second of three of that name) used his own economic muscle to make a private protest against the trade. He owned a business dealing in timber, vast quantities of which were needed by the builders of the slave ships. But Rathbone steadfastly refused to let a single plank leave his timber yard if he thought it was going to be used in the construction of such vessels.

But the big name in the anti-slavery campaign, at least as far as Liverpool was concerned, was William Roscoe. Born in, or very close to, a public house (the Old Bowling Green in Mount Pleasant in 1753) this Liverpool lawyer was a man of many intellectual interests. He was no mean linguist (he studied Italian, Latin and French) he also had a keen interest in art and was an accomplished, although amateur, botanist. At the age of 16 he left the school in Paradise Street where he had been introduced to the rudiments of education, and was articled to a firm of solicitors, qualifying as a barrister in 1774.

A man of gentle manners and thoughtful cast of mind, Roscoe at an early age appreciated the iniquitous nature of slavery. This was, after all, the age of Enlightenment, when concepts of freedom and the dignity of man were commonly discussed and written about by thoughtful men throughout Europe. But it probably did not escape Roscoe's notice that just a few miles away from the south coast of England, on the other side of the Channel, the French Revolution was being fought in the name of freedom at the same time as English merchants were up to their necks in enslaving Africans.

Somewhat unexpectedly, considering the opposition talk of abolition caused among many who feared for Liverpool's future as a trading port if slavery were abolished, Roscoe was elected Member of Parliament for the town in 1806. But his career as a politician was short-lived. For supporting the Bill to abolish slavery he was greeted by an angry mob on his return to his native town. He withdrew from political life more or less on the spot and retired to his house in Toxteth to spend his declining years writing poetry and indulging his interest in botany. In the few short months he was involved in politics, by his single act of speaking out against slavery he made more of a contribution to humanity and freedom than many who spend a lifetime sitting in the Palace of Westminster.

Slavery ended in 1807 and Liverpool did not fall apart. The dire warnings of the Jeremiahs did not come to pass; in fact the port went from strength to strength. But when passions cooled and even the most fervent supporters of slavery came to realise that it was not the respectable trade they had thought it was, it was still not easy to shake off the past. In fact it was, and still is, well nigh impossible. All around Liverpool there are still reminders of how the port grew to be the commercial giant it is today.

Take, for example, the street names. Anyone looking at a street map of Liverpool today has the whole history of the slave trade laid out before him. Significantly, however, there are far more streets named after the slave traders than there are those named after abolitionists. Bold Street and Tarleton Street are both named after merchants who made personal fortunes out of slavery at the same time as they brought revenue into the port. Blackburne Place was named after John Blackburne, who lived there in 1780s, and also made a fortune from selling slaves. He was a native of Orford, near Warrington, and Great Orford Street is also named in his honour. Not only was he an assiduous and successful slave trader, but also, as a sideline, made a name for himself trading in salt. When he moved his salt refinery to Garston, the powers that be decided to name yet another street after him, Blackburne Street.

Great Newton Street, off Brownlow Hill, is named after John Newton, already mentioned as the slaver-cum-parson who gave us 'Amazing Grace' and other well-known hymns. While he was plying his trade between Liverpool and the Americas he captained the ship called *The African*, owned by one Joseph Manesty, now remembered in Manesty's Lane, off Hanover Street. Oldham Street and Oldham Place are named after James Oldham, the captain of another slave ship who is thought to have built and paid for the first house on Oldham Street.

Sir Thomas Johnston, sometime Mayor of Liverpool and one of the prime movers in the building of Thomas Steer's dock, also had his hands in the slave trade. He part financed one of the first slave ships that sailed from Liverpool in the latter part of 1700. He is remembered in Sir Thomas Street and his son-in-law, Richard Gildart (three times mayor of Liverpool in the eighteenth century) who was also a prominent member of the slave-trading fraternity, has given his name to Gildart Street which runs off London Road.

Down near the water's edge there are two streets whose names recall geographical rather than family names. Norfolk Street has no connection whatever with the sleepy county in East Anglia. It is named after Norfolk, Virginia, a port where many of the slaves were set ashore after their journey across the Atlantic. And Jamaica Street is a reminder that cargoes such as rum and sugar often filled ships' holds on the return voyage once the human cargo had been deposited in the West Indies.

When we turn our attention to the 'abolitionist' street names the list is much shorter. There is Binns Road, named after Dr Jonathan Binns (1747–1818), a Liverpool doctor who was one of the original group who decided that something had to be done to bring the immoral commerce to an end. In Wavertree, Rathbone Road recalls William Rathbone, the abolitionist timber merchant, and his country retreat, the Greenbank Estate, is remembered in Greenbank Drive, Greenbank Lane

Liverpool Town Hall in 2007, as seen from Castle Street.

69

The grand staircase inside the Town Hall – guaranteed to impress any visitor.

and Greenbank Road. Nearly all the other places in Liverpool connected with the abolitionists are associated with William Roscoe: there is Roscoe Street, Roscoe Lane and the Roscoe Memorial Gardens. Less obviously, there is Birchfield Street, which commemorates Birchfield, the name of one of Roscoe's houses, and another which he owned, named Bentley, is celebrated in Bentley Road in Toxteth.

But it is not just the street names that bear witness to Liverpool's involvement in the slave trade. Many of the fine buildings for which the city is renowned owe their very existence to the fortunes earned by the businessmen, ship owners, captains and jolly jack tars who made handsome incomes from the ignoble commerce. The debt that Liverpool owed to the 'African trade' was summed up by actor George Cooke, who was hissed by the audience one night as he walked onto the stage of a Liverpool theatre in a state of almost total intoxication. His reply to the audience's reaction was to stand proudly erect, look them straight in their collective eye and tell them that he had not made the arduous journey to Liverpool to be hissed by the denizens of a town whose buildings were cemented with innocent Negroes' blood.

St George's Hall, the Picton Library, the John Brown Library and many of the imposing structures around the business part of the city were erected, directly or indirectly, on the strength of profits from slavery. Martin's Bank (now Barclays Bank) in Water Street and the frieze on the entablature of the new Town Hall (rebuilt after a disastrous fire in 1795, and more or less the building we know today), show

Carvings at the entrance to Barclay's Bank in Water Street graphically depict how and where many Liverpool merchants gained their wealth.

images of Neptune, elephants, tigers and little black boys holding moneybags, all of which symbolise the fortunes earned by sailing across the seas to enslave vulnerable, defenceless Africans. Unfortunately, the Town Hall frieze is too high above ground level for people to notice unless it is specifically pointed out to them, and few people stop to consider the images carved into the stonework around the entrance into Martin's Bank. They are probably too concerned with their own financial matters as they enter and exit the grand portals to take an interest in the significance of what they probably see as nothing more than unusual etchings. That is, if they notice them at all.

Meanwhile, elsewhere . . .

1750	Publication of Gray's *Elegy written in a Country Churchyard*
1751	Robert Clive captures Arcot, India
1752	Gregorian calendar adopted in Britain
1757	Clive captures Calcutta and is victorious at battle of Plassey
1759	British Museum opens
1761	John Harrison solves the problem of determining latitude
1766	Britain occupies the Falkland Islands
1770	Captain Cook lands in Botany Bay
1776	*The Decline and Fall of the Roman Empire* by Gibbon is published
1781	William Herschel, astronomer, discovers the planet Uranus
1785	Steam first used to drive the machinery in a cotton mill
1791	The *Observer* first published, Britain's oldest Sunday newspaper
1793	First £5 note issued by the Bank of England

10

EXCITING TIMES

For anyone interested in the history of Liverpool, the last few years of the eighteenth century read like a swashbuckling tale of derring-do straight out of a *Boy's Own* annual. If a young Liverpool lad in those far-off days fancied his chances as an adventurer, there was plenty of scope for realising his dreams. There was always the slave trade for those who were not too troubled by their consciences, but for those of a more thoughtful and sympathetic outlook on life there was no shortage of alternative careers. There were wars to be fought, revolutions to get involved in and, only slightly less exciting, there were new trade routes opening up in all corners of the globe which demanded to be constantly fed with fit, young bodies ready to do a hard day's graft in return for a life of adventure. And if freebooting or privateering was the way a sailor chose to make a fast killing, then there was a constant supply of ships in the harbour just waiting for prospective bounty hunters willing to sign on.

In the last half of the eighteenth century it was possible for an ordinary sailor to undertake a few privateering trips and, if luck was on his side, amass enough money to eventually become master of his own ship. There were rich pickings out there for those willing to take a chance.

Until the horrors of the First and Second World Wars in the twentieth century, the longest period of warfare which involved most of the known world was between the years 1756 and 1815. During this time, most of Europe, India, Africa and America were involved in conflict of one degree or another and Britain and her colonies were among the leading protagonists. At one point the analogy with the twentieth century could be taken a stage further: England found herself in arms against America and the combined might of France, Spain and Holland all at the same time. Added to this there was the later threat of invasion by Napoleon's troops, which made the comparison even closer. Only the players were different; the invasion threat and feeling of the nation having its back to the wall were identical, and it was only the eighteenth-century version of the 'blitz spirit' that saved these islands. And Liverpool, as in 1941, bore much of the enemy's fury and contributed greatly to England's salvation.

Privateering was really nothing less than government-sanctioned, legalised piracy. In times of need various kings, queens and governments had relied on the privateers to bolster their frequently undermanned regular navy in the defence of the realm. In the sixteenth century, Queen Elizabeth I had relied on such seafaring fortune hunters as Francis Drake to do much of the navy's work in keeping the Spanish galleons away from these shores; if they got involved in a little private enterprise at the same time, that was considered their business and the Queen was more than willing to turn a blind eye. By the middle of the eighteenth century, it is reasonable to suppose that the defence of this land might have been put on a more regular footing, but this was not the case. This was still a time when, if it looked as if the God of War intended a visitation to these shores, king and country had to rely on the ordinary citizen to do more than just his bit. We have already seen how the pressgangs haunted almost every port in England on the lookout for able-bodied men to swell the navy's ranks, and to these we can add the privateers. Unlike those pressed into service, likely lads who wanted a taste of adventure as well as a chance to earn some money could sail away and engage the enemy wherever they found him. If they came out of a skirmish as the winner, considerable fortunes could be had, as the usual practice was for the bounty to be divided into three: a third to the ship's owner; a third to the captain and the remaining third was divided up among the crew. It may seem as though the division of the spoils was somewhat unbalanced in favour of the owner and captain, who walked away with what was very much the lion's share, but such were the pickings to be had that even a share of the crew's portion could be a very tidy sum. And there was always the possibility of becoming the captain of a vessel, like Fortunatus Wright, a Liverpool-based privateer who no doubt was the idol and role model of many a boy who could not wait to sail the seven seas and, like him, return to his home port as a local hero. No doubt they would have wished to emulate his exploits in the Mediterranean, where he was reputed to have wrought havoc and captured no fewer than forty-six French ships. The booty from such a haul must have been considerable.

No less a figure in the pantheon of privateers was one William Hutchinson (born in Newcastle in 1716) who served as mate aboard Fortunatus Wright's ship and later was to achieve fame and fortune and go down in the history of Liverpool as one of her most famous sons. And his fame was due in no small part to the role he played in a skirmish with the French during the Seven Years' War (1756–63), the telling of which equals many a rip-roaring eighteenth-century tale of piracy, buccaneers and adventures on the Spanish Main.

In June 1757, Hutchinson sailed out of his home port on the ship which bore the same name, the *Liverpool*, on the lookout for French shipping to attack and plunder. He had only been out of port for a week when he encountered a much larger French vessel which ought to have proved a serious problem for the *Liverpool* but did not. After a short sea battle, the smaller captured the larger ship and Captain Hutchinson returned home with the French ship as a trophy of war and all its crew as prisoners. Not wishing to rest on his laurels, the good captain turned his ship around and set out to sea once more, this time releasing a British ship from under the French guns at Ushant off the coast of Brittany and, having watched her set a course for home, he sailed off to cause even more damage to French shipping in the southern Atlantic. He now teamed up with another privateer and the two became very much a force to be reckoned with. One daring deed the captains of the two ships devised almost beggars belief in its audacity and intended means of execution: they devised a plan for sailing right into Bordeaux harbour and attacking ships whilst they were still at their moorings. Before they could carry out their plan, however, three French ships appeared and threatened to upset the captains' plans. But, totally undaunted by the arrival of the enemy's overwhelming firepower, the two British ships captured the three French ones and then parted company. The second privateer accompanied the French vessels back to Kinsale in Ireland, while Hutchinson went off in hot pursuit of yet another three French ships he had spotted on the horizon. Amazingly, he captured these as well and escorted them back to Liverpool.

Many captains might have decided at this point that they had had enough. After all, Captain Hutchinson had probably amassed a not inconsiderable nest egg from his escapades to date and nobody could have claimed that he had not 'done his bit' for his country. But retirement seems to have been the last thing on his mind. After a well-earned rest, he started to get itchy feet and yearned for the smell of the salt breeze in his nostrils again. This time he set a course for the Mediterranean, where he resumed what was fast becoming a serious habit. He captured another three French ships in quick succession, and then news began to filter through of what perhaps was the greatest coup of his career: he captured and sold a French privateer in Sardinia for an enormous sum of money. Then he seized and sent home to Liverpool two Dutch vessels returning from the West Indies and packed to the gunwales with commodities, which no doubt included rum and tobacco. As if all this were not enough, Hutchinson himself then returned home escorting yet another French ship (a privateer the same size as the *Liverpool*) to add to his impressive list of battle trophies, which was never surpassed among the privateering community. In recognition for his outstanding career, William Hutchinson was appointed Dock Master at Liverpool in 1759 and later, in 1794, he published a treatise on seamanship in which he passed on much useful advice, based on what he had learned from Fortunatus Wright and his own experiences, to future generations of sea-farers. He died in 1801.

But Captain Hutchinson's successes were balanced by the nation's failures. Hutchinson may have enjoyed a remarkable success rate in dealing with the enemy, but that does not mean that the French did not have their moments of glory. On the contrary, they certainly did. In 1758, for instance, a daring young French privateer, Captain François Thurot, started to make life very difficult for ships entering and leaving the Mersey. He developed the tactic of lurking in the waters around the Isle of Man and plundering virtually at will. Such was his fearsome reputation that when the valiant William Hutchinson offered to raise a squadron of ships and do battle with the Frenchman, sailors were more than just a little hesitant and lacked a certain enthusiasm for the job. By the time men and ships were ready to set sail and seek out their foe, he was nowhere to be found. Like the sea mists that envelop Liverpool in the cold days of winter, Thurot just seemed to have evaporated when things began to warm up for him. It was not until early in 1760 that this irksome French sea-borne bandit was finally seen off, but not before he had given British shipping in general, and Liverpool shipping in particular, a severe mauling.

But the end of Thurot was not the end of Liverpool's misfortunes at the hands of a foreign privateer. During the American War of Independence, a certain Paul Jones proved to be no less of a nuisance than his French counterpart. British history books record this gentleman as an American privateer, but his origins were far closer to home. He was actually born John Paul in Kirkcudbrightshire, Scotland, on 6 July 1747, the son of the gardener of the Arbigland estate. From a very young age he was fascinated by the sea and made his first voyage as a professional sailor on a slave ship in 1764, but was so disgusted by the trade that he abandoned it at the first opportunity.

He turned out to be such a naturally gifted sailor that he was appointed captain of his own ship at the unbelievably young age of 21. But he was also something of a flawed genius and his enviable maritime talents were as nought when it came to controlling his violent temper, which, on at least one occasion, got him into serious trouble. In 1773, when he was in the West Indies in command of the *Betsy*, he found himself faced with a mutinous mob who demanded an increase in wages. The details of what happened during the confrontation are a little hazy, but at some point John Paul drew his sword and killed the ringleader. He probably would have argued that he acted in self-defence, but he did not hang around long enough to put his conviction to the test; he fled to Virginia and changed his name to John Paul Jones in an effort to make detection by the authorities more difficult.

When the American War of Independence flared up Paul Jones, (as he now styled himself) sided with the colonists. Within a very short space of time his little indiscretion in the Bahamas had been forgotten and he found himself a senior officer in the embryonic American navy. In April 1778 he began terrorising shipping in the Irish Sea and capturing or destroying British vessels in home waters. Then, just to remove any lingering doubts on the part of the British about his military capabilities and prowess, he sailed into Whitehaven on the Cumbrian coast and destroyed several ships at anchor, as well as one of the two forts guarding the harbour. As Whitehaven was only a mere hundred miles or so north of Liverpool, this escapade caused havoc among the townsfolk. Then, to make matters worse, when news reached the town that Jones had also captured HMS *Drake*, a 20-gun sloop, off the Irish coast at Carrickfergus, panic set in and the Council insisted that the town's defences had to be built up as a matter of urgency.

Fortunately, Liverpool's defences were never put to the test. Jones continued fighting naval battles for his adoptive country, but no longer in the vicinity of Liverpool. Then, in 1781, he returned to America where he spent the rest of the war advising how best to build up the American navy and train its officers. Hence the man who was known in Britain as a pirate and fugitive from the law was praised as a hero in the newly emerging, independent nation and is today honoured as the Father of the American Navy.

But this man's amazing career did not end there. His unequalled reputation as one of the finest naval captains the world had ever known was noted even in Russia, in 1788, when Catherine II (also known as Catherine the Great) invited him to serve in her navy with the rank of Rear Admiral. He duly accepted and served with distinction during Russia's war with Turkey (1787–92).

When John Paul Jones died in Paris in 1792 he was only 45 years old. In his short life this remarkable Scot had become a legend in virtually the whole of Europe and America, so Liverpool need feel no shame for having been put on her mettle, for however brief a time, by one of history's most formidable, if largely unsung, warriors.

The American War of Independence and the Seven Years' War with France had disastrous effects on Liverpool. The Americans harried British shipping, not only in home waters but also in the West Indies, and as trade with the former colony came to a complete halt and commerce with the Bahamas was severely disrupted, the knock-on effect in Liverpool was serious. Sailors found themselves out of work and, inevitably, as gangs of them gathered on the dockside, tempers seethed until eventually riots broke out and civil unrest became a serious problem for the Liverpool authorities. At one point, 2,000 armed mariners rampaged through the streets, terrorising the populace. Shops were sacked, public houses were invaded and the rioters even fetched a cannon or two from the ships lying at anchor in the Mersey and positioned them in Castle Street, whence they threatened to raze the Town Hall to the ground. A few cannon-balls did manage to dent the sturdy walls, but accounts of the time suggest that little damage was done and the building was saved from total destruction by, as much as anything, the drunken state of the gunners. Whether or not this is the case we cannot be certain and all we can say definitely about the incident is that the mob occupied the town for about a week, at the end of which troops were summoned from Manchester to confront the rioters and restore order.

No account of the privateers who sailed out of Liverpool in the eighteenth century would be complete without a mention of the *Carnatic*. This was a French ship captured and brought back to port laden with untold riches under circumstances which are the stuff of a comic book action tale.

The story goes that one of the town's carpenters, a certain Peter Baker, decided that he would turn his hand to shipbuilding. He set about building what he hoped would be the first of many ships and managed to gather together enough creditors to see the project through. Everything seemed to be going well until the vessel, the *Mentor*, was almost finished and his creditors got their first sight of her. All funds were withdrawn as soon as they set eyes on the monstrosity, as even the most hardened landlubber could see that the ship was totally unseaworthy. Baker now started to panic and was dogged by fears of ending up in a debtors' prison.

He hurriedly mustered a motley crew and the *Mentor*, listing heavily to one side, slowly set off down the Mersey and out into the Irish Sea, hoping to capture a glittering prize. And, to everyone's utter amazement, this is precisely what she did. The *Mentor* had not been at sea long when she encountered the *Carnatic**, a French East Indiaman low in the water with a cargo of gold and diamonds. A brief skirmish ensued, during which the French crew put up very little resistance, and within a few weeks of leaving Liverpool to the jeers of the people standing on the offing, the *Mentor* returned to the cheers of the townspeople and the peal of church bells. No doubt such a welcome had been orchestrated by those who had lent Baker money and were now going to see a good return for their investment. The bounty was valued at an absolute minimum of £135,000, which, considering the date was October 1778, was a stratospheric sum and one which gave a tremendous boost to the economy of the town. Baker's personal fortune from the adventure was sufficient for him to build a large residence which he named Carnatic Hall, with enough funds left over to add the old manor at Garston to his list of real estate acquisitions. But not even spending on this scale was enough to exhaust his bank balance, and when he died in 1795 Baker was still a rich man. Small wonder that the youth of the day viewed privateering as a career worthy at the very least of serious consideration!

In the dying years of the eighteenth century, Liverpool, England and the rest of Europe had their eyes firmly fixed on one country: France. The revolution of 1789 and subsequent events that overtook the country shook the rest of Europe and indeed the world. Ideas of liberty and social justice spread throughout the known world and people in the most remote corners of Europe eyed events in France at first with wonderment and then with apprehension. The great Liverpool reformers such as Roscoe, Rathbone and Currie greeted developments over the Channel as a chance for many of society's wrongs to be righted and for the ordinary people here and elsewhere to stand up and force the ruling classes to take note of their demands. But as the revolution sank into bloody carnage and excessive revenge on those whom the revolutionaries regarded as their erstwhile oppressors, opinions here began to change. Whig ideas on the rights of Man lost much of their attraction as the populace in general began to feel that the British constitution and traditions were under threat. In Liverpool, the Tory Member of Parliament, a rich landowner named Bamber Gascoyne, retained his seat at the elections and a kind of collective paranoia gripped the town. Anyone with foreign connections, interests or tastes was immediately suspected of traitorous, revolutionary intentions. A small group of Liverpool enthusiasts who met irregularly to spend a pleasant evening together discussing Italian literature over a glass or two of wine were forced to abandon

---

*   The ship took its name from Carnatic, a region on the south-east coast of India. It was an area where, in the eighteenth century, the French and English engaged in what came to be known as the three Carnatic Wars.

their harmless, if somewhat academic, pastime. An interest in anything foreign was immediately construed by a nervous population as conspiratorial intentions pursued under the guise of innocent relaxation.

But we should not be too hasty in condemning the nationwide paranoia. Napoleon (who overthrew the Directory in 1799) was on the rampage throughout Europe and so it is little wonder that the authorities in Britain saw an invasion of these isles as a possibility. And towns such as Liverpool would have been particularly edgy; the war against Napoleon was being waged mainly at sea, so all ports would have been on particularly high alert. It was only after Nelson's defeat of a combined Spanish and French fleet at the Battle of Trafalgar (1805) that port authorities could afford to relax their guard a little when hostilities switched mainly to the land. Napoleon continued to be the scourge of Europe for another decade, suffering major defeats only at Moscow (1812) and then, finally, at Waterloo (1815) where the British, under the command of Wellington, together with the Prussians under Blücher, finally crushed the Corsican Corporal.

It was perhaps because of these seemingly interminable European wars and campaigns that England took her eye off the ball as far as America was concerned. She probably assumed that after the American War of Independence there was nothing more to worry about from over the Atlantic. She probably thought that her former colony would quietly slip into the background and get on with the business of recovery and recuperation after the war with her erstwhile rulers. But England was mistaken. In 1812, another Anglo-American war broke out, a war which is largely forgotten on this side of the Atlantic, probably because it was regarded more or less as something of a sideshow, as the military might of England at the time was more concerned with what Napoleon was planning next than the shenanigans of some backwoodsmen half a world away. Unfortunately, this was a serious error, as the inadequate forces sent out to deal with the Americans (many of whom thought they were fighting a second war of independence) got something of a bloody nose. There were no victors in the war, as both sides had their successes and failures in roughly equal measure. When peace was restored in February 1815 – by the signing of the Treaty of Ghent – neither side had gained anything worth mentioning and all that was achieved was a restoration of the *status quo ante bellum*.

Nevertheless, this rather pointless, forgotten war did have consequences for Liverpool. It would have been an act of suicide on a mass scale for the emerging American navy to take on the might of the British navy in open battle; she would have been out-classed and out-gunned at every turn. So the American commanders took what they considered to be the only course open to them: they brought back the privateers. And this they did with conspicuous success. Their huge, well-armed ships plied the waters of the West Indies and inflicted serious damage on British trading ships, many of whom would have been bound for the port of Liverpool. Then, not content with the losses they were inflicting on British ships on the other side of the Atlantic, the privateers turned their attention to the coast of Africa, and even the coastal waters of Britain herself. One ship in particular, the *True-blooded*

Yankee, took up a position in the Irish Sea and, for two whole years, plundered ships at will as they approached or left Liverpool.

The 1812–15 war was the last fling for the privateers. The end of the war ushered in a period of peace which allowed Liverpool, England and Europe as a whole to breathe again and by the time of the next major war the practice of privateering had been either outlawed or at least brought under strict international control. Relations with America had also begun to improve and Napoleon Bonaparte was no longer a festering sore on the exhausted, war-weary body of continental Europe. So, with slavery and privateering consigned to history and the country at peace, the likely lads from Liverpool who sought a life of adventure and the adrenalin rush of danger had to look elsewhere. There was still excitement to be had from sailing to foreign climes, but looming on the horizon was also the unstoppable onrush of industrial expansion and development which was about to grab the country by its vitals. And for those looking for an outlet for their superfluous energy there would be no shortage of opportunities to expend their youthful vitality. New industries, new inventions and discoveries (as well as new applications of old ones) were to channel the aspirations of all in directions they could never have imagined.

Meanwhile, elsewhere . . .

1795 Consumption of lime juice made compulsory in the Royal Navy as a prevention against scurvy

1796 Spain declares war on Britain

1797 Death of the political thinker Edmund Burke

1798 Suppression of a rebellion in Ireland

1798 Nelson defeats the French fleet at the Battle of the Nile

1799 Income tax introduced as a temporary measure to raise war funds

1799 Royal Military College, Sandhurst, founded

1800 First shipment of the Elgin Marbles arrives at the British Museum from Athens

11

OF MEN & MACHINES

A s the clock struck midnight on 31 December 1799 and people toasted the advent of the new century in the lowliest of taverns and the grandest of houses throughout the land, wishes would have been expressed for 1800 to be a more propitious year than 1799. Rough pewter tankards and glasses of the finest crystal alike would have been raised as hopes were intoned for greater health, prosperity and happiness for friends and family in the coming year. But few of those enjoying the New Year celebrations would have realised the full extent of the changes that were about to engulf the country as a whole, and Liverpool in particular. As we have seen, every century ushered in changes, some minor, some major, which had an effect on Liverpool's social fabric and physical landscape. But the nineteenth century saw such a confluence of historical development, scientific advances and population redistribution that it can rightly be claimed that the 1800s were the time which saw the greatest changes of all. The Industrial Revolution had been gathering steam since the previous century, when mankind really began to take charge of nature and harness her awesome power. From time immemorial he had sought to control natural forces, but his attempts had been crowned with only minimal success. Now, however, he was on the verge of being able to tap into elemental forces in a manner which would allow him to replace muscle power with machinery on a grand scale. And the advantages were obvious: muscles grow tired and weak as men grow old; machines by comparison seem to go on and on forever. Men demand wages, housing, time off when they are ill, and can inconveniently die unexpectedly at any moment. They can also cause trouble by joining trade unions, demanding a decent standard of living and having ideas above their station. But machines do as they are told, and as long as they are fuelled and kept in good repair they continue to churn out artefacts without question and without making unreasonable demands on their owners. Of course there had always been primitive machines of one sort or another, but in the years straddling 1800, mankind learned how to build colossal engines which could, and would, make a significant difference to the means of production in the coming industrial age.

The hope was that the new inventions and discoveries of the previous century would find ever-wider application and thus make life easier for all. But the reality was that, as we have already seen, far from being set free from the hard grind of physical labour, the vast majority found themselves enslaved to the machines, factories and factory owners who now dominated the industrial landscape. Trade would, in future, be conducted over ever-increasing distances over an ever-decreasing timescale, and people would move in greater numbers than ever before from one part of the country to another. And as factory owners realised how profits could be vastly increased by the use of new machinery, their concerns for the welfare of their employees diminished.

As these social dynamics gathered momentum, Liverpool, with its strategically dominant port facilities, was at the very heart of the revolution. It was perhaps the only place in the realm which could cope with the vast increase in the transportation of goods and people which characterised the opening years of the nineteenth century. And one of the first tasks that landed on Liverpool's doorstep, both literally and metaphorically, was how to deal with the influx of people coming from Wales, Scotland and Ireland, some of whom merely used the port as a transit stop on their way to settle in America, whereas others never intended going any further and yet others just ran out of money and had no choice but to make Liverpool their new home.

Just how momentous a change this influx of new blood into the borough caused can be seen from a brief look at the population statistics. In 1792 there were about 60,000 people living within its boundaries – twice as many as had lived there in 1760. By 1831 the population had shot up to 165,000, and the results of this human explosion were twofold: new housing had to be erected as quickly as possible and new land had to be acquired to accommodate it. This was the era when we begin to see what was soon to become a regular feature of the landscape: vast housing projects in places such as Everton, Walton, West Derby and Toxteth began shooting up in a desperate attempt to keep up with the ever-increasing number of residents who needed adequate shelter. Not that the new housing could by any stretch of the imagination be referred to as sumptuous. This was an age when factory owners would build basic housing for their workers near the factory, not for reasons of messianic altruism, but because they needed the workforce close at hand. Hours were long (a 72-hour week was not unusual) and the work was arduous, so all that was needed was a place where men (and women and children) could do little more than get shelter for the night and then return to work before the sun was up the following day. Hence the nineteenth century witnessed a mushroom-like growth in cheap, basic housing, offering minimal space and even less comfort. The result was mile after mile of terraced houses, which later became the working-class slums.

Liverpool had always been a pluralistic town. We can be quite certain of this because the town rolls, dating back to just a few years after the founding of the borough, contain a fair number of English, Welsh and Irish surnames intermingled with those of descendents of the Norman French who came over with William the

One of several Irish pubs in the city. It's a pity the Gaelic greeting over the door is misspelt!
The word 'fálte' should be 'fáilte', the Gaelic for 'welcome'.

The sign over the entrance to the pub known locally
as 'Pogue Mahone's'.

There's a warm Irish
welcome for anyone
looking for 'good craic'
in this establishment.

Anyone who needs the loo in this pub has to learn at least a couple of words in Gaelic! 'Mná' is the 'ladies' . . . and 'fir' is the 'gents'.

Conqueror. In the last years of the eighteenth century, many came to settle from Wales, Scotland and Ireland as the new industries provided opportunities for work which simply did not exist at home. But it was the potato famine in Ireland of 1845 that caused the greatest influx of Irish into Liverpool. Even today, over 160 years later, evidence of the immigration from Ireland can be seen throughout the city centre. There are pubs whose names hark back to 'the old country' littered all around the city centre, not a few of which offer the Gaelic welcome above their doors to all who seek liquid refreshment within. Just a few hundred yards from Lime Street station, travellers seeking rest and recuperation after a long journey are greeted with 'Céad míle fáilte', the Irish for 'a hundred thousand welcomes', over the entrance to the Liffey pub. And just a moderate leg-stretch from there is another pub, which has to be an Irishman's joke on all monolingual Englishmen. At the top of Seel Street, which runs parallel to Bold Street, stands a hostelry known locally as 'Pogue Mahone's' and the universal assumption is that at some time in the past an Irishman named Pogue Mahone opened the pub as a meeting place for homesick Irishmen working or living far away from the Emerald Isle. But the truth is that Pogue Mahone is really the Gaelic 'póg mo thón' (pronounced pogue mahone), which means 'kiss my bum', skilfully manipulated to look like the pub proprietor's name and simultaneously have a joke on the English.*

Despite its Irish connections, Pogue Mahone's is not situated in the Irish part of the city. When immigrants began to arrive in considerable numbers, most of them settled around the Scotland Road area, principally because it was reasonably close to the docks where many Irish found work. With the redevelopment of the city and greater wealth and mobility of its citizens, Scotland Road has now lost much of its

---

* Strangely this same joke has been played on the people of Chicago and Milan, where there are establishments of the same name.

84

character and 'Irishness', a development which can be seen both as a good thing and as a bad thing. The tight-knit community spirit has largely disappeared; the urban geography with a pub on every corner in which many a weekly wage disappeared on a Friday night before its owner had crossed the threshold of his lowly abode, has long since changed beyond recognition. And the doorsteps, scrubbed spotless with a 'donkey stone', at the entrance to houses where visitors would always find a 'welcome' on the mat have now largely passed into the 'Scottie Road' folklore of local historians and Liverpool's balladeers. Thankfully, however, we have also witnessed the disappearance of the grinding poverty of the times when the immigrants arrived hoping for a better life only to find one not much better than the one they had left in Ireland. At its worst, the poverty and privations endured by the people of Scotland Road were so bad that eighty per cent of children born in the area died before the age of 10. Housing conditions were dreadful and most people who lived in the area eked out their miserable existence crowded together in tiny houses with no running water or proper sewage. Unsurprisingly, when 116,000 Irish men, women and children arrived from the west coast of Ireland in 1847, the conditions were perfect for disease, particularly typhus, to run riot through the community. Accurate figures of the infection rates are impossible to obtain, but we do know that something in the region of 60,000 immigrants were treated for

A memorial in the grounds of St Luke's Church, written in English and Gaelic, in memory of the Irish who perished during the great famine of 1845–52.

typhus, and a further 40,000 for diarrhoea and dysentery. In 1847 alone, no fewer than 2,303 people were buried in the graveyard attached to St Anthony's Church. The cemetery has now gone, but there are still thought to be 1,200 Irishmen lying at peace in the church crypt.

Wack and Wacker

Until fairly recently, this was a very common form of address among natives of Liverpool, as well as an epithet used to designate residents of the city by those who were not. Few dictionaries bother to include the term and those who do usually state that the origin is unknown. But I would venture the following explanation.

The nineteenth-century Irish immigrants were mostly Gaelic speaking and in Irish the word for son is 'mac', as in the prefix to many surnames where it means 'son of . . .'. Now in Irish, if we wish to change 'son' to 'my son' we have to write 'mo mhac' which is then pronounced 'mo wack'. 'Wacker' would simply have been a local variation.*

But it was not only the Irish who added such a powerful ingredient to this cultural melting pot. It is not generally realised, but Liverpool contains the oldest Chinatown in Britain. From the middle of the nineteenth century, diminutive Chinese sailors could be seen, no doubt to the amusement of the locals, walking through the dock area and even further afield in the more central parts of the town. Of those who came as a result of the growing trade between England and China, some stayed, for one reason or another, and thus an Oriental flavour was added to an already varied mixture. And the new enterprising immigrants spotted what must have been a gap in the market. They soon realised that sailors of all nationalities passing through the port needed accommodation, and so they established boarding houses where sailors and other itinerants could get a bed for the night at a reasonable cost. They also noticed another opportunity for making a healthy living: laundries. The people who stayed in their nineteenth-century B&Bs might occasionally want their clothes to be washed and the Chinese obliged. But it was not only the travellers who needed clean clothes. Very few, if any, of the houses in Liverpool would have had even the basic facilities needed for washing clothes, and the advent of laundries must have been a boon for those who could afford to take advantage of the service they offered.

It has been estimated that at its height the laundry business employed over 25 per cent of the Chinese community. In the 1930s the numbers of Chinese in the city began to decrease, and consequently the establishments offering laundry facilities also began to tail off. Then, by the 1950s, when housing conditions had improved

---

* See *Word Routes* by Alexander Tulloch, published by Peter Owen, 2005.

*The Chinese Arch, completed in 2000, near Nelson Street. The inscription says 'jung gwo cheung',
Chinese for 'China Town'.*

*Many street names in this part of the city are written in English and Chinese, but few capture the
spirit of the Orient the way this one does, lit up on dark nights by a genuine Chinese lantern.*

Another example of English/Chinese street signage.

immensely and washing machines were just starting to become a feature of domestic life, the new generation of Chinese turned to catering. This was post-war Britain and a new generation was growing up with a more adventurous outlook on life and increasingly more disposable income in their pockets. In the 1960s, Chinese restaurants seemed to spring up on every street corner and so rapid was the growth in the popularity of Chinese food that soon they began to supplant many of the old traditional fish-and-chip shops that had provided a staple diet in Liverpool since the 1850s. The 'Chinese takeaway' had arrived and it is still with us today.

In a sense (although it probably was not realised at the time) the massive influx of immigrants was something of a blessing in disguise. The new engineering projects, which had been gathering momentum since the previous century, now exploded in a fury of expansion. And chief among them was, without doubt, the railway. There had been primitive attempts at marrying carriages up with parallel lines along a given route between two points for many years, but the first time locomotion was achieved by successfully harnessing steam was in the early 1800s, and the first railway to connect two cities was that between Liverpool and Manchester in 1830. It had not been an easy ride, either literally or metaphorically, as the creation of the railways as a means of conveying passengers and freight had been fraught with what many at the time believed to be insuperable problems. There was a great deal of opposition from interested parties, such as those who earned a living from the toll roads and canals; Lord Sefton was horrified at the thought of dirty, smoky, noisy trains blighting the landscape near to his estates, and many Mancunians (renowned for their frequently radical political ideas) were opposed to the project simply because they thought it would give the ruling classes further excuse to exploit the toiling masses. Surveyors at the Manchester end of the line were frequently subjected to stone-throwing mobs and consequently the work was delayed by several months, if not years.

In addition to this human opposition, there were other problems from a far more implacable, unyielding source: the geology and geography of the land. In order to overcome the natural obstacles offered by the lie of the land, the engineers had to strain every nerve of ingenuity in their bodies, and the labourers were forced to sweat blood in an effort to lay track over the mere thirty miles that separated the two towns. And it was in this all-consuming need for sweated labour that the immigrant population was to play such a vital role. Machines had made headway in reducing the need for muscle-power, but they had not replaced it completely and the enormous tasks that lay ahead in the construction of the world's first railway soaked up immigrant labour, most of it provided by hundreds, if not thousands, of Irish navvies, on a scale which had probably never been seen before in Britain.

There are two indispensable parts to a railway: there has to be a track constructed in such a way as to prevent derailments, and there has to be a reliable engine (or locomotive as they were originally known) to pull the carriages.

So the first thing to do was to design a locomotive. Throughout the 1820s all sorts of ideas and theories had been flying around about how best to generate the power that would pull the carriages. One bright spark thought of having enormous cables at one end of the line pulling the train from the other. Another thought that it would be sufficient to have the carriages pulled along the lines by teams of horses; in other words, a glorified stagecoach on rails.

For the more serious designers and engineers several days of trials were held at Rainhill, just under twelve miles from Liverpool, in October 1829, where the would-be kings of the railway were able to demonstrate their wares. But stringent conditions were laid down for all entrants: (1) the maximum weight for all locomotives was 6 tons; (2) all wheels had to be mounted on springs; (3) the cost of each locomotive must not exceed £550; (4) the gross weight of the carriages plus the winning locomotive had to be at least three times the weight of the locomotive; (5) the winner would have to demonstrate a speed of not less than 10mph; (6) the winner would also have to demonstrate reliability.

Numerous designers and engineers initially showed interest in the competition, but in the event only five showed up on the day with their creations. There was the Sans Pareil, the Rocket, the Novelty, the Perseverance and the Cycloped. Of the five, the Cycloped, either by accident or design, turned out to be the fun element of the competition. Something between 10,000 and 15,000 people are reported to have turned out to see the competition, and they must have roared with laughter when the Cycloped began to show what it could do. This strange contraption consisted of a horse positioned on a platform and walking on a drive belt, which was supposed to deliver enough power to propel the carriages. Obviously it failed miserably; not only did it reach a maximum speed of only 5mph but the horse suddenly fell through the floor of the platform, bringing the train to a sudden and definite stop.

Three of the four locomotives left were plagued by breakdowns of one sort or another. Perseverance fell off its conveyor wagon on the way to the trials and was so seriously damaged that its owner spent five days trying to repair it. When it did finally make an appearance it only reached 5mph. The Sans Pareil made a promising start but then one of its cylinders developed a crack and so it had to be withdrawn. The lightest and smallest of the entrants, the Novelty, achieved a creditable 28mph on the first day, but on the second the boiler nearly exploded and faults appeared which simply could not be rectified within such a short period of time. So it, too, was disqualified, and the winner was Robert Stephenson's Rocket, which had satisfied all the requirements, out-performed the opposition and demonstrated that the future was bright for railway transport not just in Liverpool or Britain, but also throughout the world. So Robert Stephenson and his Newcastle-based firm were awarded the £500 prize money and a fat contract with the Liverpool and Manchester Railway Company.

But this was the easy part. Now was the time for the really hard work to begin. The man had been found to build the locomotives and all that was needed was a line to run them on. It was the civil engineers' time for glory, even though the problems that faced them were enormous. But they did it. The combination of explosives, picks, spades and sheer ingenuity triumphed in such a magnificent manner that in September 1830, less than a year after the Rainhill trials, the Liverpool–Manchester rail link was opened.

It had been decided after numerous surveys, conducted in a atmosphere of acrimony and argument, that the best route would be to leave Liverpool and take a vaguely northern route through Fazakerley, and then swing south through Croxteth, and then head east by way of Knowsley, St Helens, Leigh and Eccles, and finally terminate in Salford. This route avoided the greater gradients of the land on Liverpool's outskirts, but it did not solve the problem caused by the authorities, who had stated categorically that the line must not cut through any of the built-up area spreading out from the town centre. This meant that three tunnels had to be constructed at the approaches to the terminus. Also, no fewer than fifty bridges had to be built, and it was further stipulated that the line had to either go over or under the turnpike roads lying in its path. When the engineers (and the navvies!) came to

Olive Mount just outside Liverpool, they were faced with millions of tons of solid rock that had to be cut through in order to form a cutting which would allow a sufficiently low gradient for the early locomotives to cope with. They blasted away what they could, but it still meant that almost half a million cubic yards of rock had to be shifted by navvies working with little more than shovels and their bare hands. Then came the Wapping Tunnel, another job that required technical skill of the highest order and weeks of blood, sweat and tears. But when it was completed, rather than just leaving it as an enormous gaping hole in the hillside, it was decided to engage the talents of the architect John Foster to finish it off with a Moorish arch.

The next two problems the engineers faced were the Sankey Valley near St Helens and the infamous Chat Moss. The Sankey Valley problem involved building a huge viaduct consisting of nine arches 60ft off the ground and spanning the Sankey brook and canal. Then came what many people thought would be the engineers' nemesis: Chat Moss. This is a vast stretch of peat bog covering about twelve square miles to the north of the River Irwell and lying directly on the route which the railway was intended to take. Had it been a normal run-of-the-mill stretch of marshland it still would have presented problems, but of a totally different kind and magnitude. The Chat Moss bog is comprised mainly of a spongy vegetable growth covering an enormous area in which one year's growth of moss appears to climb over the previous year's, without the previous growth rotting away completely. This, apparently, causes far greater problems for engineers, as it cannot be solved by normal drainage techniques.

George Stephenson, the chief engineer on the project, had recruited another engineer, John Dixon, to help find a solution for the bog problem. Between them they devised a plan they thought would work. First of all they laid a footpath of heather across the marshland, following the proposed eventual route of the railway track. The footpath seemed to work so well that it was reinforced and widened, and then a temporary railway track was laid out across it to see if it could take the weight of a one-ton wagon. This was only partially successful. It worked fine where the bog was relatively shallow, and it allowed the 200 men working on the project to drain a substantial area of land. But where the marsh was deeper the technique was almost totally useless and Stephenson and Dixon now had to change tack. They scratched their heads and chewed on their steel-nibbed, dip-in pens as they tried in vain to come up with a solution. Then a certain Robert Stannard, who was also working on the project, came up with an idea for a firm but flexible track. This involved laying thousands of timbers in a herringbone design, intermeshed with heather and brushwood hurdles, to form a bed on which the railway track could be laid. They tried it and, to everybody's amazement, it worked. The problem had been solved and, even though progress was still slow, the Rocket hauled a wagon weighing one ton across Chat Moss on 1 January 1830. Nine months later, the line between Liverpool and Manchester was officially opened with a great deal of fanfare and rejoicing. But the day was marred by a terrible accident. The MP for Liverpool, William Huskisson (who was also President of the Board of Trade), walked across the tracks to exchange a few words with the Duke of Wellington who was also attending the ceremony. He did not hear the Rocket heading down the track in his direction until the very last minute, by which time it was too late. In an attempt to get out of the locomotive's way he tripped and fell, one leg going straight under one of the Rocket's wheels. Frantic attempts were made to save him but to no avail. He died a few hours later. It was a tragic end to a glorious beginning of a new era. But the Doubting Thomases had been confounded and all the difficulties which might have persuaded lesser men to give up their dream had been solved. There was now nothing to stand in the way of progress; the Railway Age had truly arrived.

Once the railways were firmly established as a viable means of transport there was no stopping them. Within a few years, virtually all the major towns and cities throughout the whole country had been linked up to a vast network of lines spreading out like a gigantic cobweb. But it did not end there. It was soon realised that if railways could provide fast and efficient travel between places like Liverpool, Manchester, Birmingham and London, why should a modified form of the train not perform a similar service within towns and cities? And it was such thinking that led to another revolution in public transport: the tram.

The first horse-drawn trams started operating about 1859/60 and then, in 1866, the Liverpool Tramway Company came into being and, starting in Castle Street, laid what was to be the first lines in a network which would eventually extend out over the whole town. Dingle, Walton and Aigburth had all been connected by 1871. In 1898 electrification of the lines began and by 1901 the horses, which had performed such sterling service for so long, were put out to grass. Consequently, people now found themselves scurrying about between different parts of the city (as Liverpool was designated by Royal Charter in 1880) on their trams and between towns and cities all over the country by train, enjoying a freedom of movement their parents and grandparents could have never imagined. But the dreamers and planners were not finished yet.

Scarcely had the visions of these wondrous new forms of transport been made a reality than some in Liverpool began to raise their eyes, quite literally, to the heavens. If trains could run over viaducts 60ft above the ground for part of their route, surely they could travel a mere 16ft or so above ground for the whole length of their route? The original proposal for such an 'overhead railway', proposed in 1852 by John Grantham, was rejected by the Mersey Docks and Harbour Board. But in 1877 the Board had another look at the plans. Once again the members decided that it was just not feasible financially, and so the plans were shelved. But another engineer, George Lyster, whose imagination had been fired by the idea of an elevated railway running along the Liverpool shoreline, put his plans forward for consideration in 1882. Yet again it was a lack of funds that prevented the plans getting off the drawing board. But Lyster persisted and finally, in 1887, a bill was passed in Parliament which meant that the plans could go ahead and so work finally began in January 1890. The Overhead Railway (soon universally referred to as the 'Dockers' Umbrella' because those who walked to work could shelter under it on

A 1950s view of a train on the Overhead Railway.

The 'Dockers' Umbrella', as seen from one of the streets leading up from the Pier Head.

A typical Liverpool tram: a popular, if noisy, form of public transport until 1957.

rainy days) opened three years later and was an immediate success. Running as it did for almost the whole length of the docks from Dingle to Seaforth, a total distance of just under seven miles, it became a favourite among the dockers who travelled on it to and from work. But it also became a tourist attraction and as late as the 1940s and early '50s dads still queued up to give their young sons an experience which few boys anywhere in the world could enjoy. The carriages were crowded and smoky, the windows were dirty and the seats, made of hard wooden slats, were very uncomfortable. But none of this mattered to the wide-eyed youngsters as they gazed down on the mighty ships in dry dock and then stared up at the mammoth cranes towering over the whole scene like monsters from a prehistoric age. For a small boy, a trip on the Overhead Railway had a dream-like quality to it and was guaranteed never to be forgotten.

Sadly, the Overhead Railway did not stand the test of time. It had been in operation for little more than forty years when it first began to show serious signs of deterioration. Pollution, rain, and no doubt the salt air blowing in from the Irish Sea had taken their grim toll on the iron structure. It soldiered on until the 1950s, but by then the damage was irreparable and in 1956 it was decided that the whole structure

Trams on the Pierhead, 1947. (Sutton Collection)

had to be dismantled. By 1959 the breakers had done their work and what had been such a boon to the city was no more. And if that were not enough, 1957 was also the year when the faithful old trams, now deemed too outmoded for the modern age, clanked and screeched along Liverpool's thoroughfares for the last time. The city was suddenly deprived of its most iconic forms of transport which, for a whole generation of Liverpudlians, now became no more than a receding memory.

Meanwhile, elsewhere . . .

1801	Nelson wins battle of Copenhagen
1801	First census of Great Britain conducted
1805	Scott's *Lay of the Last Minstrel* published
1809	Dartmoor Prison opens
1810	Luddites makes their appearance
1813	Jane Austen's *Pride and Prejudice* published
1817	Jane Austen dies
1821	*Manchester Guardian* on sale for the first time
1837	Queen Victoria ascends the throne
1849	Cock fighting banned as a spectator sport
1861	Post Office Savings Bank opens

12

CONTRASTS

Slavery, sugar and tobacco, the Industrial Revolution and the advent of the railways made Liverpool rich, fabulously rich. Money poured into the city from all over the world so fast that by the middle of the nineteenth century the 'fat cats' of the day did not know what to spend it on. Building projects were undertaken on a lavish scale; grand houses were built for the rich entrepreneurs who had done much to create the wealth, and the development of the city showed no signs of slowing down.

But not all benefited. The dreadful, destructive poverty, which had always been such a feature of Liverpool's history, showed little if any sign of disappearing as the heavenly manna descended upon a privileged section of the community. The moneyed classes, who had so much cash at their disposal that they could probably have solved the slum problem with little more than a wave of the hand, chose not to. They preferred to spend their riches on grandiose, magnificent buildings, which would ensure them a place in history as benefactors who had helped create one of the most opulent cityscapes in Europe, if not the world. We can now gaze in awe at many of the architectural wonders clustered around Liverpool's city centre, but we should also ask ourselves how the poor felt when they saw these magnificent buildings sprouting up around them. As they sat and starved in their freezing hovels, watching their children die for want of a few pence, what must have gone through their minds as they saw kings' ransoms being lavished on architectural wonders to which they would never have access? The neglected souls who died in their hundreds of cholera, typhus and just plain hunger in their pathetic cellars a mere few yards from where architects strove to outdo each other in the magnificence of their creations are now just statistics. The forgotten and neglected are long gone; but the creations that brought ancient Athens and Rome to the banks of the Mersey are still there to impress visitors and make Liverpudlians glow with pride, at least in the beauty of their civic buildings if not in the social conscience of those who commissioned them.

When the partygoers at the New Year celebrations welcomed in the nineteenth century, the area around modern William Brown Street, Lime Street and Renshaw

Street was the edge of the countryside. London Road was still little more than a country lane flanked by fields where a farm labourer, chewing on a juicy wisp of straw as he rested from his toil, might have turned an inquisitive eye to watch the odd stagecoach hurtling past. But by the time the partygoers' grandchildren were old enough to throw a delinquent stone or two at the stagecoach, things were very different. Much of the land had been yielded up to make way for some of the most beautiful examples of revival Classical architecture to be seen anywhere in England.

The jewel in the crown of Liverpool's architectural wonders has to be St George's Hall and it owes its very existence to music. It had been decided by the authorities that a suitable venue was required for the triennial music festivals (the first being held in 1784) that took place in the town. The Town Hall, which had previously played host to such musical extravaganzas, was deemed too small for the swelling ranks of the leisured classes who sought enlightened, cultural entertainment. Thus an

St George's Hall in 2007.

architectural programme was undertaken which would alter the shape of the north side of Liverpool forever.

When some of the leading dignitaries of the town decided (in 1835) that a new assembly hall of sorts was needed for the ever-grander musical performances Liverpool was putting on, they were able to raise the magnificent sum of £25,000 and the city council promised to let them have the old infirmary site for their new venture, should it ever show signs of getting off the ground.

The next step was to find an architect, and it was decided that the best way to do this was to hold an open competition. A young strip of a lad in London, one Harvey Lonsdale Elmes, heard about the competition and submitted his plans. No doubt he was as amazed as anybody else when he won; he was only 24 years old. Coincidentally, a year earlier Liverpool had been designated an Assize Town; this meant that a building suitable to house law courts had to be built in the town. Elmes also won the contract to design this building, and so, in order to minimise the costs, it was agreed all round that one building should be built which would be grand enough to accommodate civic festivals, concerts etc. and also courts of law.

There was to be nothing modest about the new building. Elmes was instructed that not only must it be suitable for the activities for which it was being designed, but it also had to reflect the growing pride the city fathers felt in their successful trading town. This was an instruction the young architect gleefully fulfilled in his plans; as his starting point he took no lesser buildings than Westminster Hall and St Paul's Cathedral in London. And he was not going to leave any room for doubt as to the edifice's purpose in the minds of those who would later survey his wonderful creation: artibus, legibus, consiliis (to arts, laws and councils) was his chosen inscription over the southern entrance, proclaiming to all who entered that this was a building dedicated to the finer aspects of civilised existence.

Unfortunately Elmes died before his creation was completed. Work began in 1841 and was completed in 1854, but young Elmes died in the West Indies in 1847 and so the work on his architectural masterpiece had to be continued by others under the supervision of Robert Rawlinson and John Weightman, the Corporation Surveyor. In 1849 the architect C.R. Cockerell was engaged as a consultant and then, in 1851, he was appointed chief architect to oversee the final stages and eventual completion of the task. The final cost of St George's Hall was £290,000.*

We can only surmise that if Elmes were to come back to Liverpool today he would not be disappointed; his brainchild is magnificent. St George's Hall is a fine example of neo-Classical architecture, standing proud on a modest elevation and looking over the broad sweep of St John's Gardens to the south and flanked by the

* Just to put this figure into perspective, readers might be interested to know that a recent (2006) refurbishment cost something in the region of £23 million.

A view of St John's Gardens behind St George's Hall.

The Wellington Column erected in memory of the Iron Duke. It was designed by George Anderson Lawson of Edinburgh and towers 132ft over Lime Street.

Wellington Monument (erected 1861–3), the Picton Library (1875–9), the William Brown Library (1857–60) and the Walker Art Gallery (1874–7). Viewed from a comfortable distance, this cluster of neo-Classical buildings provides what has to be one of the most beautiful examples of urban scenery in the country.

But there is a symbolism about St George's Hall which is seldom, if ever, mentioned. Contained within its walls are a civil court and a Crown court, as well as assembly rooms capable of accommodating grand concert performances, balls, festivals and all manner of public entertainment. And an observer blessed with just a scruple of Attic salt might have noted that the one edifice catered both for the rich and influential on the one hand and for the less fortunate on the other. One end of the building was used by the favoured classes of society for their lavish entertainment and the other end for trying and passing sentence on those who were forced into a life of crime in order to survive. We can easily imagine that, in one half of the building, a judge might have sentenced a man to a lengthy prison sentence for nothing more than stealing a loaf of bread to feed his family and then gone home to get ready to attend a civic function in the other half in the evening. The social divisions of Liverpool were made flesh under the one roof.

Those city luminaries who employed Elmes to design a building which would reflect the port's maritime and trading glory paid little if any heed to the conditions of those who lived in the abject poverty that characterised many Victorian towns and cities. From the relative comfort and affluence of the twenty-first century, it must be almost impossible to imagine the hardship suffered by the majority of the populace in the Liverpool of not all that long ago. We have already seen how housing was almost swamped at about this time by a sudden influx of immigrants from other parts of the country and from Ireland, and it does no harm to point out that it was not until the 1950s that any substantial measures were taken to improve the situation. And of course the overcrowding, unspeakable poverty, the lack of regular employment (the biggest employer, the docks, employed men on a day-to-day basis) and the almost total absence of anything resembling an efficient police force, created the perfect conditions for crime. And if we factor in an added dimension, alcohol, the picture gets even worse. It has been calculated that something like every seventh building in Liverpool in the early eighteenth century was engaged in the sale of alcohol, and the situation remained more or less the same until the 1870s. A moderate amount of ale or even whiskey might have been used to lubricate the odd Irish ceilidhe down by the docks or on Scotland Road, but more often than not, strong drink was also the cause of street brawling, domestic violence and even riots and civil unrest. There were parts of the city where a pedestrian always had to be careful and take adequate precautions against the Victorian era's equivalent of today's muggings. Even in broad daylight, there were areas were angels would fear to tread; but at night they were best avoided altogether. A half-hearted attempt had been made in 1811 to establish some degree of policing in the town, but it was almost totally ineffectual.

Ceilidhe

This is another example of a linguistic import from Ireland into Liverpool. It is the Gaelic word for a 'visit' and is derived from the word 'ceile', meaning companion. It was originally used to describe an evening when friends would gather together to listen to poetry and music and then have a bit of a dance. Interestingly, it is also the origin of the Liverpudlian's term for someone who has over-indulged and is only fit to be described as 'kaylied'.

We have already seen how, in cases of extreme rioting, armed soldiers could be ferried in from other towns such as Manchester to deal with the Liverpool mobs, and no doubt this was a resource still at the disposal of the authorities before more capable forces of law and order could be established. It was not until 1837 that anything approaching a viable police force was created in Liverpool, and even then it was not intended for the protection of citizens of the whole borough. The Liverpool Police Force, as it was officially known, did operate a round-the-clock service, but for the first five years of its existence its 'manor' did not include the area around the docks. This part of town was considered just too dangerous. The combined forces of visiting sailors, drunk on testosterone and cheap ale, and the thieves, prostitutes and pimps who had a vested interest in keeping the area lawless, could make life very difficult for any uniformed busybody who tried to enforce the law of the land there.

This, then, was Liverpool in the second half of the nineteenth century. There was opulence, wealth and culture. But there was still the appalling squalor, brutishness and a certain degree of anarchy that had characterised her social profile since her founding back in the thirteenth century. Feral children roamed the poorly lit streets in Victorian Liverpool, as they had done in previous centuries, on the prowl for someone to rob or food to steal. And the care taken by some in planning the port's physical appearance had not been reflected in the borough's consideration for its less well-off citizens. But there was a glimmer of hope. The later years of the century saw the beginnings of improvements which would eventually give virtually all Liverpudlians a better life. Yes, progress was slow, very slow, and it took many years for the improvements to filter down to those at the bottom of the heap. But a start had been made and that is what matters.

Arguably, the most important single development which led the way to better social conditions was water. Even today, there will be people still alive in Liverpool whose grandparents would have remembered the days when not every household enjoyed the benefits of a plentiful supply of clean, running water. In the years spanning 1842 to 1864, certain benefactors, philanthropists and men of science and medicine stressed the importance of decent housing for the health of the community as a whole. But it also gradually dawned on people that there was little point in building brighter, more commodious houses if there was no reliable and plentiful supply of water. Until the mid-nineteenth century, the people of Liverpool had to rely on wells, streams and probably just plain rainwater for their supply. Bootle and Toxteth Park wells had been particularly important as their waters were clean and of very good quality, but the quantity of their beneficence was less than adequate. In fact, the flow was so poor that water was only available to the majority of Liverpudlians for between fifteen and thirty minutes per day. In the very poor areas (the ubiquitous Liverpool courts, for example) several families would have to rely on a single standpipe. We can just imagine the scene: a family member would be deployed to wait by the standpipe, whatever the weather, with a jug or bucket in hand, praying for the water to be turned on. And he or she would not be alone. There would be others waiting, pushing, jostling and probably even fighting to be first in line and to make sure he or she did not return home empty-handed. And woe betide anyone who dropped the precious nectar between standpipe and home; even a single drop spilled would almost certainly have been cause for severe reprimand.

Under such conditions it is not surprising that personal hygiene and laundry was not all that high up on a family's list of priorities. When water is scarce, the first thing to do with it is drink it. It's no use having clean clothes and a clean face if you are dying of thirst. But this is the choice many people would have had to make, although it has to be remembered that in Liverpool, as in the rest of the country at the time, beer and ale were drunk as a substitute for water.

In 1852, work began on the construction of a reservoir in the area surrounding Rivington, just to the north of Bolton, and by 1857 clean water was flowing into some (but still not all) Liverpool homes, and for the first time since the founding of the borough the supply was plentiful and constant. There was just one fly in the ointment; the engineers who had brought about this modern-day miracle had underestimated how popular the innovation would prove to be. And so, in 1880, another massive feat of engineering was begun, this time to pipe water all the way from Lake Vyrnwy in mid-Wales to Liverpool. And this is where the city still gets most of its water from today.

The contrasts in Liverpool at the time were not only social. By the end of the century and the early years of the next, Liverpool entertained contrasts of an entirely different order. There was the commercial heart of the city and there was the almost anarchic thuggery of the dockside area, and it is fair to assume that in neither of these quarters would intellectual or spiritual concerns have played a significant role in the daily lives of the people. Soon, however, Liverpool was to acquire an intellectual life and a spiritual life centred around two architectural additions to the city: the University and the Anglican Cathedral.

This idea of creating a university in Liverpool was not met with anything approaching unfettered enthusiasm when it was first mooted. In fact, when Charles Beard (who had been one of the leading lights at the School of Medicine since its foundation in 1834) first suggested that a University College should be set up in the town, few would even entertain the idea. There was scarcely anybody of wealth, power or influence in the town who had not gained his or her wealth, power or

Church Street in 1898.

influence through trade, and their attitude to life was generally moulded by financial concerns. If a project did not have an obvious and immediate commercial value it was not worth considering. Their concept of a university was such that they envisaged healthy young men idling their time away studying arcane, unmarketable subjects such as Latin and Greek, Theology or Philosophy, and this was not an image that appealed to them. They certainly would not have wanted to spend any money on an institution that encouraged such pursuits.

Fortunately, there were a few who thought otherwise. A certain Bishop Lightfoot (himself a Liverpool boy) and William Rathbone, the celebrated philanthropist, could see nothing but benefits in having an institution in the town which offered learning and higher education to the bright young things (provided they could pay!), not only from Liverpool but from further afield as well. At first they met with the same lack of interest and distinctly tepid enthusiasm as Charles Beard had met. But gradually they began to change minds and, eventually, Liverpool Corporation came round to supporting the idea, and so schemes were devised for raising the funds. By 1882, enough cash had been raised and a University College was established. But even at this juncture we can only assume that the enthusiasm for a seat of higher learning was not as great as it might have been. Without any sense of irony, those in authority deemed that the most suitable place for the new institution was to be a disused lunatic asylum situated in a run-down part of the city. And even after the University College became a fully-fledged university in 1903, it appears not to have occurred to anyone that a position with a less inauspicious history might be more suitable. Brownlow Hill is still the home of Liverpool University today.

Then there were the purely spiritual considerations. Liverpool had never suffered from a dearth of churches. Right from its earliest days, when it was a far-flung corner of the parish of Walton, it had a church, St Mary of the Key, by the water's edge and then in the eighteenth century, churches seemed to grow like mushrooms as the town spread its borders further inland. So in 1880, when Liverpool became a diocese in its own right, thoughts naturally turned to building a cathedral. But construction did not begin until 1904, when Edward VII laid the foundation stone, and it was not completed until 1978. This might seem a long time, but the undertaking was enormous both in terms of architectural challenge and financial cost, although the result was another magnificent edifice on the Liverpool skyline. In striking contrast to the Classical splendour of St George's Hall, the Anglican Cathedral stands like a mighty Gothic sandstone sentinel looking down with

St Nicholas's Church on or near the site of the ancient chapel of St Mary del Key.

dignified austerity on the city, the port and the ships that come and go. In fact, it is universally recognised as being one of the finest (if not the finest) examples of twentieth-century Gothic Revival architecture in the country, which is all the more remarkable when we remember that Giles Gilbert Scott was only 22 years old when he submitted the plans that won the open competition organised by the city fathers in their search for an architect.

But the design an observer of the Cathedral sees today is not the design which won the competition. Right up to his death in 1960, Scott could not resist the temptation to alter his original ideas, and arguably the most dramatic change that he introduced involved the roof. Originally he had planned to crown his creation with twin towers, one over each transept. But then he had a change of heart and decided on a single, much taller central tower (331ft high) and this produced the unmistakable configuration of the Cathedral as we know it today. Sir John Betjeman, poet and renowned expert on church architecture, had no hesitation in deeming it 'one of the

The Anglican Cathedral as it appeared in 2007.

greatest buildings of the twentieth century' and there are few who would disagree. It is the largest cathedral in the UK, the largest Anglican cathedral in Europe, and boasts the heaviest peal of bells (31 tons). Inside, few visitors fail to be impressed, as they look upwards, by the highest and widest Gothic arches to be found anywhere in the world. The mighty organ is also the largest in the world, with no fewer than 9,765 pipes.

Once construction had started and the Cathedral began to rise above the rooftops, it must have seemed to observers as though the borough had reached its pinnacle; its development was about to be rounded off and completed. The trinity had been achieved and the city could boast a commercial centre, a university and a cathedral. The residents of Liverpool could now look to the future secure in the knowledge that, whatever Fate had in store for them, the institutions were in place to care for them in body, mind and soul. And this is just as well; in the twentieth century, Liverpudlians' bodies, minds and souls were to be sorely tested.

Meanwhile, elsewhere . . .

1863	London's underground opens (the first in the world)
1865	Publication of Lewis Carroll's *Alice in Wonderland*
1868	TUC founded
1872	*Marie Celeste* found adrift in Atlantic
1875	Captain Webb first person to swim the Channel
1877	Wimbledon hosts first Lawn Tennis Championship
1878	The *Liverpool Echo* established
1880	Publication of first telephone directory in England
1883	Karl Marx dies in London
1897	Bram Stoker's *Dracula* first published
1900	Death of Oscar Wilde

13

THE URBAN PHOENIX

Take a stroll along today's Lord Street, drop into a city-centre pub or trendy wine-bar, go and watch a football match or spend some time down at the Pier Head on a fine summer's day and take a look at the people around you. The vast majority of them will be well, even stylishly, dressed; they will be well-fed, healthy-looking and will show little sign of being short of money. But there have been times in the last hundred years when the picture you behold would have been a very different one. For the first three decades of the century the political and economic vicissitudes of Liverpool would have been reflected in the unmistakable signs of abject poverty, desperation and feelings of abandonment. Added to this were the disastrous effects of two world wars, the second of which, in particular, came unbelievably close to reducing the city to nothing more than a pile of rubble. In fact, there is something almost biblical about the trials and tribulations endured by the citizens of Liverpool at various times during the twentieth century; it is as if the Four Horsemen of the Apocalypse liked the place so much they had decided that if they were not going to take up permanent residence in the city then at least they would visit it on a regular basis. But no matter what misfortune befell Liverpool, no matter what calamities history rained down on the city, its people always came back fighting and it arose time and time again from its own ashes. In fact, considering how resilient the Scousers proved to be, particularly during the first half of the twentieth century, perhaps it is time for the Liver Bird to stand down and make way for the Phoenix as the city's iconic symbol.

It would be more than just a touch naïve to imagine that the serious social divisions which characterised Liverpool in the closing years of the nineteenth century and first years of the twentieth could continue without repercussions of one sort or another. Sooner or later the deprived underclass were bound to demand, if not the whole cake, then at least a bigger slice than they had enjoyed hitherto. They could see that a small minority at the top controlled most of the wealth of the city, and in 1911 some of the have-nots decided that they could tolerate the situation no longer and made their feelings known to those who had ignored them for so long.

The spark that set the flame alight was a refusal by the ship owners to recognise the dockers' rights to be members of a trade union. No doubt feeling that their wages and working conditions were so poor that they had nothing much to lose anyway, the dockers went on strike and made their way to St George's Hall, where a rally was to be addressed by the Labour activist Tom Mann. Support for the strike was so solid that not a ship moved in or out of Liverpool; the ship owners had visions of their businesses and profits disappearing before their very eyes and so they gave in. Not only did they agree to allow membership of trade unions, but offered no resistance to the demands for better pay. But the dockers, fired up by their victory and no doubt more than just a little intoxicated by heady feelings of power, still refused to go back to work and called for other workers on the railways and trams to come and join them. The matter was now out of the hands of the ship owners; the city authorities (and probably the government also) detected a whiff of revolution in the air and decided on firm action. At first the local truncheon-wielding bobbies were sent in to deal with a crowd of workers who had gathered in front of St George's Hall. If contemporary accounts are accurate, the crowd retaliated by hurling bricks and stones at the police, and what had been no more than 'a little local difficulty' developed into a full-scale riot. Hundreds were injured as the fighting raged for three or four days and the authorities by this stage were now

The 1911 strike committee with Tom Mann, the leader, sitting in the second row from the front, fourth from the left.

The police arriving in force to break up the 1911 riots.

seriously worried. European revolutionary fervour was the last thing they wanted
on British soil; drastic measures had to be taken, and so a Royal Navy gunboat was
positioned in the Mersey at the same time as the troops were sent to confront the
mob. Two rioters were killed in the ensuing fracas, but the riot was ended and the
workers agreed to return to work.

By a strange quirk of fate, however, this was not the end of civil unrest on the
streets of Liverpool. Eight years later, in 1919, there was more rioting in the centre of
the city when some of the lowest paid workers in the whole country decided that it
was their turn to demand more pay and better working conditions. The irony of the
situation this time, however, was that the workers who were making these demands
were none other than Liverpool City Police. In a classic reversal of the poacher-
turned-gamekeeper situation, the police, many of whom no doubt had beaten the
rioters of 1911 about the head with their truncheons, now found themselves making
exactly the same demands as their former victims. And, of course, many of the
populace took advantage of the situation. With the police on strike, looters were
able to go on the rampage with impunity and this is exactly what they did. Hardly
a shop window escaped the rioters' attention and it is more than likely that nobody
ever knew the full extent of property and goods that simply 'disappeared' into the
rarified atmosphere of the Liverpool slums.

It seems, however, that the police lacked the commitment of the dockers of 1911 and so their strike was soon over. But the conditions were slightly different, as the police chose to go on strike at a time when the country was recovering from one of the bloodiest wars in history. It just might have occurred to some of them (or, perhaps more accurately, it was pointed out to them) that it was rather unpatriotic to inflict rioting and looting on a population that was still suffering the effects of the First World War. On the other hand, the government, mindful of what Lenin and his Bolshevik revolution had recently achieved in Russia, probably made it very clear that they had no intention of countenancing similar disruption and opposition in Britain.

When the war ended in 1918, Britain, along with the rest of Europe, America and Russia, was in a parlous state. Millions of young men had been sacrificed in Flanders Fields and in other theatres of war, and the politicians vainly proclaimed that the conflict would be 'the war to end all wars' and that the soldiers who survived would return to, in Lloyd George's words, a 'fit country for heroes to live in.' They had answered the call, gone off to fight for King and country and deserved only the best that their homeland could offer them. But within a very short time after the Armistice, the politicians' glib platitudes must have had a very hollow ring to them as the boys returned to find that what awaited them was little better than what they had left behind in 1914.

At the outbreak of the war many young men in Liverpool were as keen as any to go and fight. Promises of a short war which would be 'over by Christmas' and which would give the young blades a chance to come home covered in medals and glory was just too tempting for them. Any who hesitated were shaken out of their indecision by recruitment campaigns typified by Kitchener's 'Your country needs you' posters and the white feathers handed out by women to any young men who seemed less than enthusiastic for the fight. In the event, despite an understandable nervousness experienced by some, thousands of Liverpudlians volunteered and sailed off to the killing fields of the Somme, Ypres, Passchendaele and countless other hell-holes in a war that tore Europe apart. Something in the region of 15,000 of Liverpool's sons never returned.

Liverpool's unique strategic position meant that the city became the headquarters for the Western Approaches and as such played a vital role in the defence of the nation's shipping. It also meant that she was a prime target for the Kaiser's navy and, in particular, the submarine fleet. It did not take a genius to work out that a German U-boat in the Mersey could wreak dreadful economic damage on Liverpool and the whole country if it attacked merchant shipping moored in the river. And, furthermore, a few sunken merchantmen in the Mersey could make life very difficult, if not impossible, for the military planners who used Liverpool as a port of embarkation for troops sailing to France and Belgium.

But there is one event of the war with which Liverpool is associated and which is always quoted in history books as an example of German ruthlessness and stupidity. On 7 May 1915, the 32,000-ton Cunard passenger liner Lusitania was nearing the end of a voyage from New York to Liverpool and was just a few miles off the Irish

The Lusitania Memorial.

coast, close to Kinsale. A German U-boat spotted her and attacked; at 1.20 p.m. her torpedoes hit home and the Lusitania sank within twenty minutes. Of the 2,500 people on board, over 1,000 died, nearly all of them civilians. But the Germans paid a heavy price for their 'gallantry' as over a hundred of the passengers who perished were American citizens. This single act of ill-judged militarism is usually thought to have been a contributing factor in America's decision to join the war on the side of Britain and her allies. If this is true, the German High Command must have rued the day when one of their U-boat captains sank an unarmed ocean liner. It has to be said, however, that Germany has always maintained that it had no choice in the matter; America was illegally transporting arms and ammunition to Britain and the reason the ship sank so quickly was because, after being torpedoed, a secondary explosion blew the ship apart. And the only explanation for such a massive explosion was that it was caused by the shells illegally concealed in the hold.

Whether or not the *Lusitania* was carrying armaments we shall probably never know for sure. What is beyond doubt, however, is the effect the news of the sinking had on the populace of Liverpool. Many of the *Lusitania*'s crew and her captain came from Liverpool, and as soon as the news of the sinking reached home people spilled out onto the streets, screaming for revenge and venting their anger on anyone who had connections, however tenuous, with Germany. Shops known to belong to Germans were trashed and their contents looted. But, alarmingly, when the baying mob had exhausted its supply of German victims, it turned on any foreigner it could get its rabid claws on; refugee Russian Jews were attacked, as were Chinese laundries, and their inoffensive proprietors beaten up. The much vaunted cosmopolitanism and racial symbiosis of Liverpool were shown to be, at least as far as some of the population were concerned, little more than a veneer.

After the signing of the Armistice in November 1918 the soldiers began to come home, but it was not to the brave new world they had been promised. They had won the war but it had not been an easy victory. They had been through hell and were quite right to expect some sort of appreciation for the sacrifices they had made during four long years of conflict. But they were in for a shock. After the initial fanfare and joyous, flag-waving homecoming for the survivors and pious words for the dead, harsh reality set in. The slums were still there; people still eked out a miserable hand-to-mouth existence; soup kitchens opened for the thousands of jobless and many limbless ex-servicemen begged on Lime Street for whatever passers-by would grudgingly give. Unemployment in the 1920s was such a serious problem that the government seemed totally incapable of solving it. Then, in the '30s (the decade of the Great Depression following the Wall Street Crash), things went from bad to worse. Nobody was able to come up with a solution, and Liverpool Council's attempt to at least make an effort to alleviate the housing difficulties came up with a policy which was so ill-conceived and short-sighted that it beggars belief. It embarked on a council house building programme which was, in theory, a laudable project. But where did they build these wonderful new houses? In places like Huyton and Norris Green, miles away from the docks where most manual

Walton Vale, Aintree, as seen from the Black Bull, c. 1920.

workers were employed, if and when there was any work for them to do. So a docker, transplanted to one of these outlying areas would be faced with a problem every day: should he spend what little money he had to travel in to dockland in the hope of getting a day's (or even just half a day's) work? If work was available, his tram fair would make a sizeable dent in his pay, but if there was no work at all he would have spent his fare on a wasted journey. And it wasn't only the manual workers who suffered from unemployment. The thousands of clerks who moved bits of paper around in offices also lived in fear of losing their jobs. Men would sit at their desks and pretend to be checking ledgers or writing letters to non-existent clients and having telephone conversations with imaginary customers, just to look busy. The alternative was to let your boss see you twiddling your thumbs or tapping your desk with an otherwise unemployed pencil: if that happened it could mean joining the dole queue.

But vast, soulless housing estates with no shops and few amenities of any kind, built miles from where people need to be in order to earn a living, were not the only building projects undertaken in Liverpool in the first few decades of the twentieth century. Despite the chronic social and economic problems which continued to dog the whole country and Liverpool, the money and the will could always be found to build imposing buildings which reflected the city's trading prowess and prestige, even at times when that prestige was on the wane. In addition to the Anglican Cathedral, begun in 1904, we can also add the magnificent buildings at the water's edge, known collectively as The Three Graces. The first of these to be erected was the Mersey Docks and Harbour Board (now the Port of Liverpool Authority) building, built between 1903 and 1907. Then came what was to be the most magnificent of the three, the Royal Liver Building, begun in 1908 and finished in 1911. And finally between 1914 and 1916, when the country was in the grip of the Great War, the Cunard Building made its appearance.

Even in the 1930s, when 3,000,000 men nationwide were unable to find work and Liverpool was suffering from unemployment at least as much as the rest of the country, the appetite for grand building projects did not diminish. The year 1934 saw the completion and opening of the first Mersey Tunnel (the second opened in 1971) linking Liverpool with Birkenhead. It had been built in anticipation of the increased traffic which planners thought would be the inevitable result the expansion of motorcar manufacturing in America and on the Continent. The overall cost of the project was £8,000,000, which, as it turned out, was money well spent as the expansion in car ownership was one development that the planners foresaw with remarkable perspicacity, considering the poverty and deprivation in Liverpool at the time. Many people couldn't even afford a gallon of petrol, let alone contemplate buying a car.

If the economic situation at the time seemed to offer nothing but gloom and despair, the political situation offered little that was any better. There were a few in Liverpool in the 1920s who thought Lenin's and then Stalin's Russia might hold the key to Britain's problems as well; then in the '30s Sir Oswald Mosley advocated a Fascist regime in this country modelled on Hitler's Germany and Mussolini's Italy, and gathered about him a small band of followers in Liverpool. But by and large people in Liverpool paid little attention to the events on the Continent. Far from seeing Hitler and his ilk as a saviour, most Liverpudlians appear to have understood that what was brewing on the horizon was not salvation from economic and social problems but the gathering storm clouds that could mean only one thing: war. And they were right.

When war was declared in September 1939, Liverpool was virtually a front-line city. It may have been several hundred miles form the battlefields of France and Belgium, but it was nevertheless a prime target. Hitler's generals knew that if they could destroy the port of Liverpool it would have a catastrophic effect on Britain's ability to continue the war. And it was not just Germany's navy that threatened Liverpool now; the city, along with London, Plymouth, Coventry and even Belfast, was well within the range of Goering's bombers, as the 'home front' would eventually find out.

But at first there was the period generally referred to as the Phoney War, when nothing much seemed to be happening. Picture-goers had seen newsreel film of

What was left of St Luke's Church after the May Blitz in 1941.

Stukas, Heinkels and Junkers bombing far-off places such as Guernica, Rotterdam and Warsaw, and were expecting similar horrors to be visited on them, but, in the early days at least, the skies were empty and their nights untroubled. In late 1939 and early 1940 the war was a long way away. For Liverpool it was little more than an inconvenience as people went about their business at the same time as trying to get used to carrying a gasmask, learning to live with ration books or spending a few hours a week mastering basic Home Guard skills and sewing black-out curtains. But the war suddenly seemed very close when the call-up papers fell through the letterbox and landed on the mat. Those who had listened to the politicians' talk of the 'war to end all wars' twenty years earlier now had to brace themselves again as they watched their husbands, brothers and sons marching off for a second time to fight a German foe. And of course any lingering illusion that the war was a distant horror in a far-off land was dissipated in a flash when the telegraph boy appeared on the doorstep with the dreaded telegram in his hand.

Clearing away the rubble and looking for possible survivors became a way of life for many Liverpudlians during the war years.

The bombing of Liverpool got off to a slow start. In 1940 the occasional raids caused only slight damage, and such was the inaccuracy of the Luftwaffe's bomb-aiming technology that many of the early bombs landed in the hills of North Wales or on farmland beyond the city limits. But the so-called May Blitz of 1941 was a different story altogether. The bombers came over every night for a week, starting on the 1st and ending on the 7th, the night of the 3rd being the worst. The destruction was widespread and in the space of just one week almost 2,000 people were either killed or seriously injured.

One particularly effective tactic used by the Luftwaffe was to mix 1,000lb high-explosive bombs with incendiaries. The result was that those buildings that were still standing after the thousand-pounders had done their worst were frequently swallowed up by the ensuing flames. But the effect of this combined bombing was more than the sum of its parts: the fire crews could not always reach the burning buildings because of the thousands of tons of fallen masonry now blocking the

Out of the frying pan and into the fire.

roads, and even when they did manage to get through, there was frequently no water for their hosepipes as the water mains and fire hydrants had been destroyed. They were forced to rely on the water their tenders could carry and, faced with the huge number of fires raging throughout the city, they were simply overwhelmed. The firemen, valiant as they were, could sometimes do little but stand and wait for the fires to burn themselves out; some nights the conflagration was so intense that it could be seen for miles beyond the boundaries of Liverpool. There are still people alive today in the Lancashire Fells, over thirty miles away, who can describe what it was like to stand at their back doors and stare at the bright red glow in the sky over Liverpool.

During the blitz, large areas of the city were destroyed and thousands of people were made homeless. The only choice many had was to decamp to outlying areas of the city where the chances of being bombed were relatively slight. One such area was the council housing estate at Norris Green, which had not long before

A typical example of 1930s council housing in Norris Green.

been abandoned by people who had gone there to live and so escape the crowded conditions of Liverpool's inner-city housing. But they were soon so fed up with the lack of amenities and transport that they moved back to the city slums where at least they had shops and pubs and could avail themselves of the public transport system. Now they were only too glad to live in Norris Green; they were away from the air raids and had a roof over their heads.

But it was not only homes that were destroyed in the area near the city centre. A great many commercial properties were bombed and companies were forced to conduct their business on tables set out among the rubble in the streets. And when the tramlines were blown up or the bus drivers could not manoeuvre round the bomb craters, those people who still had offices to go to thought nothing of walking miles through the rubble and broken glass and past leaking gas mains to get to work. It is a testimony to the courage and resilience of the people that very few of them thought of not going to work or of giving in. Liverpudlians just got on with it.

By the application of perverted logic, it is possible to demonstrate that Liverpool owed its continuing survival and existence to one man: Adolf Hitler. Admiral Raeder, the Commander-in-Chief of the German Navy, tried his best to persuade Hitler that for strategic as well as psychological reasons it would make sense to bomb Liverpool off the face of the earth. He argued that the total annihilation of the port and city would send a clear message to the whole country. This, he believed, would demonstrate the destructive power of the Luftwaffe and Germany's willingness to use what we now call 'shock and awe' to ensure victory. His argument was a convincing one and, had Hitler not been preoccupied elsewhere, he could have been proven right. Fortunately for Britain, if unfortunately for the Russians, the Führer was about to launch Operation Barbarossa (the invasion of the Soviet Union) and, totally ignoring Raeder, he transferred most of his aircraft to the Eastern Front.

This meant that from the summer of 1941 the bombing of British cities was minimal and inflicted only what the military referred to as 'sustainable losses'; the last bomb to fall on Liverpool killed fifteen people in Stanhope Street on 10 January 1942.* It is a sobering thought that if Hitler had not made the classic strategic error of opening a second front, the history of Liverpool might easily have come to a very abrupt end in May 1941.

There was one wartime activity in which Liverpool played a vital role but which is seldom mentioned in history books on the city: intelligence. Anyone who has had even the slightest connection with the Forces knows that one of the most important aspects of any war is espionage. This does not mean that Liverpudlians all of a sudden became suave James Bond characters haunting the Liverpool nightspots in dinner jackets with beautiful ladies on hand to light their cigarettes and smile seductively. On the contrary, Liverpool was one of the centres of real intelligence work involving painstaking, methodical research in unglamorous

---

* Unbelievably, this was the very street where Adolf Hitler's nephew William Patrick Hitler was born on 12 March 1911.

Perhaps the most famous view of Liverpool – the Liver Buildings from the river.
(Sutton Collection)

surroundings, with intelligence officers sifting through documents, maps, letters etc. in an effort to second-guess the enemy. Littlewoods offices at Edge Lane and Vernons Pools office in Aintree were commandeered by a branch of the Intelligence services whose task it was to open mail and examine it for cryptic messages and information being sent to various parts of the country and abroad. Linguists and code-breakers spent long hours in dingy offices, poring over love letters, business letters and simple greetings cards, frequently written in a foreign language, in case a spy ring was using innocuous, normal-looking mail to convey information of use to the enemy.

Just how successful these unsung heroes of the war were we shall probably never know, as details of their successes and failures have never been made public. But we do know that they earned their crust and that they did uncover some German spies (and spies from neutral countries working for the Reich) and were even successful in 'turning' one or two and using them to send disinformation back to their controllers in Germany.

When the nightmare of war came to an end in May 1945, Liverpool, as with the rest of the country, breathed a sigh of relief. As the news of Germany's unconditional surrender filtered through, crowds thronged onto the streets and headed for the centre of the city. Flag-waving, cheering, singing and dancing Liverpudlians, old and young alike, savoured the taste of victory and whatever the pubs could offer. Church bells rang out for the first time since 1939 and the cares and woes of ordinary people no longer seemed to matter. The war against Germany was over, the survivors had coped with the worst that Hitler could throw at them; nobody and nothing could beat them now.

There was still the matter of the war against Japan in the Far East, but nobody doubted that it was only a question of time before the Japanese forces went the same way as those of the Third Reich. And indeed in August, three months after Germany's capitulation, Japan surrendered too. People could not believe it, but it was true. The war, which many expected to sound the death-knell of Great Britain, her Empire and her allies, was at long last over. All that was needed now was for people to get up off their knees, shake off the dust of war and rebuild their shattered lives. But it was not going to be easy. The country was bankrupt; the task of rebuilding its infrastructure was a daunting one, and there were still many years of hardship and sacrifice ahead. But at least people could go to bed at night and not lie awake worrying about loved ones in a distant theatre of war.

Meanwhile, elsewhere . . .

1901	Death of Queen Victoria
1907	Boy Scout movement founded by Robert Baden-Powell
1908	Introduction of the Old Age Pension
1912	The White Star liner RMS *Titanic* sinks on her maiden voyage
1917	The Russian Revolution
1918	Death of the poet Wilfred Owen
1920	Founding of the Communist Party of Great Britain
1926	Year of the General Strike
1930	Airship *R101* explodes on maiden flight
1936	Jarrow to London hunger march
1939	Conscription introduced for men
1942	First broadcast of *Desert Island Discs*
1945	Labour government under Clement Atlee elected

14

NEW HORIZONS

Rising from the ashes was not easy. In fact, in some ways it was more difficult than coping with the horrors of the war as there was little if any immediate improvement to the day-to-day struggle just to exist in bombed-out cities such as Liverpool. Rationing of clothes and certain foods continued for some time after the war had ended. Bread, which had always been available if not exactly in abundant supply, was suddenly added to butter, eggs and meat as another commodity available only with ration coupons. And, as if this were not enough to contend with, temperatures plummeted and the winter of 1946/7 was one of the coldest since 1814, with snow falling somewhere in Britain every single day from 22 January to 17 March.

The Siberian blast meant that the people of Britain found themselves enmeshed in two vicious circles simultaneously, one involving fuel and the other food. It was so bitterly cold that people, naturally, had to heap more coal on the fire to keep warm and the power-stations, also fuelled by coal, should have stepped up production to cope with the increased demand for electricity. But the relentless sub-zero temperatures froze the winding gear at the pitheads and no coal could be brought to the surface. The dwindling stocks in the coal yards and at the power stations could not be replenished. The coalman's lorry became an increasingly rare sight on the streets and electricity was made available for only a few hours a day as the government attempted to conserve supplies.

At the same time the atrocious weather interfered with the distribution of food, and deliveries to shops and markets became erratic and infrequent. And if that were not bad enough, vegetables, which were never rationed and formed a substantial part of many people's diet, became increasingly difficult to find. Huge quantities of them quite simply froze in the ground. The iron-hard earth refused to yield its treasured commodity and many a shop shelf took on the woebegone look of sad abandonment. In short, as the people's need for warmth and food increased day by day, the government's ability to satisfy it decreased hour by hour.

So, all in all, the citizens of Britain had a pretty rough time: they still couldn't get enough to eat, it was difficult for them to keep warm, clothing was rationed (although second-hand clothing was exempt) and yet they had to get on with the business of rebuilding the country.

Much of the rebuilding that had to be done was purely physical; the thousands of houses, offices and public buildings destroyed in the war had to be rebuilt, and this alone was an undertaking of daunting magnitude. Many Liverpool bombsites were not even cleared of rubble, let alone built on again, until well into the 1950s, and there were still the charred remains of what had been people's homes to be seen near the city centre in the early '60s.

But there was also another kind of rebuilding going on at the same time: political restructuring. In the late 1940s Liverpool, along with the rest of the country, swung towards the Labour Party. Churchill had, surprisingly, been defeated in the first general election after the war and left-wing politics held sway throughout the country. In Liverpool a formidable firebrand politician was chosen to represent the people at Westminster and fight for the city's poor, forgotten and neglected. And fight is exactly what Bessie Braddock did best.

Elizabeth Braddock (née Bamber) was born in Zante Street, Everton, in 1899. Her mother, Mary Bamber, was an ardent socialist who wanted to make sure that her daughter grew up with an active social conscience and strong political opinions.

Zante Street, where Bessie Braddock (née Bamber) was born, as it appeared in 1959. The street's association with the sun-soaked Greek island of the same name is not immediately apparent!

To throw her in at the deep end she took young Bessie, wrapped in a blanket, to her first political meeting when she was just a few weeks old and set her off along the socialist road which she was to follow for the rest of her life. Years later, as an adult, Bessie could still describe the look she had seen on the faces of the unemployed in 1907 and remember the tears and despair in honest men's eyes when there was no more soup to be had in the soup-kitchen. Such a vision of the lower depths was a driving force throughout her political life. Then, when she was 12 years old, Bessie went with her mother to hear the workers' demands at the 1911 demonstration outside St George's Hall. No doubt the ensuing riot and scenes of truncheon-swinging policemen attacking men who wanted nothing more than a decent wage with which to feed their families, served only to reinforce her determination to rid Liverpool of the soup-kitchen and all it stood for.

Everton

In Anglo-Saxon times this part of the Parish of Walton must have been where boar were kept or wild boar were known to roam. We can safely assume this as the modern name is derived from the Anglo-Saxon words 'eofor' (boar) and 'tun' (enclosure).

Her concern for the underdog led Bessie at one point to become a member of the Communist Party, although she later resigned when she realised her mistake; the Communists had even less interest in genuine democracy than capitalists, but it was an indication of her commitment to social justice and a fair deal for the working man that she joined the party in the first place, although her own reason for such a move sounds, typically, a little more down-to-earth. She claimed that she joined the Communist Party for no other reason than that she was a rebel. And she went on to say that she left the party for the same reason once she had seen the true nature of the movement.

When the young Bessie Bamber left Anfield Road Council School at the age of 15, she was first employed as a seed packer, but later found a job in a draper's store and then moved on to get herself a job in the drapery department of the Co-op on Walton Road. But by 1921 she was already taking an active interest in politics, having discovered a flare for public speaking, which she combined with her disgust at the working and living conditions of many people in Liverpool. But her public socialism soon became a private passion as well when, in 1922, she married her sweetheart of seven years, another ardent fighter for social justice, Jack Braddock. Together they were a formidable couple on the Liverpool political scene and made their presence felt both locally and in the country as a whole.

Bessie's first step up the political ladder came in 1930 when she was returned as Councillor for St Anne's Ward, Liverpool. Then, in 1945, she was elected Labour MP for Liverpool Exchange and served her native city with distinction for twenty-four years. During her time in the House of Commons she fought valiantly as the doughty champion of many an underdog, and it is a terrible reflection of the conditions that still prevailed in Liverpool in the late 1940s that she still considered it her duty to demand decent living conditions for Liverpudlians. Despite the slum clearances of the '30s and the destruction of much of the city during the blitz, Bessie still felt it necessary to regale her fellow Members of Parliament in her maiden speech for doing nothing about the 'bug-ridden, lice-ridden, rat-ridden, lousy hell-holes' that many of her constituents had to call home.

In April 1970, 'Battling Bessie', as she was known, was awarded the Freedom of the City in recognition for the incomparable work she had done for the citizens of Liverpool. Unfortunately by this time she was not a well woman and was too ill to attend the ceremony. She died just a few months later and it is no exaggeration to say that her passing marked the end of an era. There was still much to do, but Liverpool in 1970 was a far better place to live in than it had been in 1945, and much of the improvement was down to Bessie.

We can of course only surmise what Bessie's reaction would have been to the turmoil of the 1980s, but we can hazard a pretty good guess whose side she would have been on. These were dark days when industrial strife and unemployment stalked the land again, leaving misery and desperation in its wake. The Prime Minister, Margaret Thatcher, adopted a policy of confrontation with the unions, and in particular the miners, and there was an understandable reaction from the Left. Arthur Scargill, the miners' leader, stood up to Margaret Thatcher, but lost the battle. Neil Kinnock, leader of the Labour Party, found himself fighting on two fronts: his 'official' opponent was the Prime Minister, but he also had to contend with a new power in Liverpool politics, the Militants, led by Derek Hatton, deputy leader of Liverpool Council. This was a dark period in the history of the city when the Council was taken over by a Trotskyite clique whose opposition to the government and Labour Party alike became national news. They attempted to seize and retain power by what many saw as gangster methods and this made an eventual clash with the official Labour leadership inevitable. Fortunately for the people of Liverpool, Neil Kinnock won the battle.

Although Liverpool as a port had been in steady decline since before the war, it was during the 1970s and early '80s that her fortunes nosedived. Changes in world trading patterns, industrial strife and government neglect put the city into recession. Unemployment soared as factories closed and workers once again found themselves without a job. As Thatcherism bit deeper and deeper into the veins that carried the lifeblood of Liverpool's erstwhile industrial and maritime glory, the city's landscape began to resemble a wasteland. Where industry had once thrived, business premises, factories and shops closed and were boarded up. Some were small businesses but others were long-established mighty industrial concerns that had been part and parcel of Liverpool's very existence for generations. And none was more symbolic of the city's former trading glory than Tate & Lyle, the sugar refiners. The refinery in Love Lane had provided work for generations of Liverpool families and it had become such an institution in the city that few could imagine Liverpool without it. So all the greater was the shock when the end came. In January 1981 it was announced that the factory was closing down and, ironically, the reason was Britain's membership of the European Economic Community (EEC). The Common Market, as it had originally been called, was supposed to bring great trading opportunities for the country and her industries. But it was an EEC directive that put the lid on Tate & Lyle in Liverpool. Sugarcane, refined for so long at Love Lane, was replaced by sugar beet by the EEC as the preferred raw material for the production of sugar. This move put Liverpool at a serious disadvantage as all the sugar beet was grown further south in counties such as Lincolnshire and Rutland. Of course there were protests, but these fell on deaf ears. The factory at Love Lane was deemed uneconomic and, despite the dreadful social consequences on a city already gripped by yet another round of unemployment, 1,500 men were shown the door.

Such cavalier treatment of workers and their families inevitably caused resentment and anger. The government's inability or unwillingness to side with the Tate & Lyle workers was symptomatic of its attitude as a whole. To those people on the ground in Liverpool it seemed as though Westminster, in faraway London, cared little for Liverpool and for the city's workers even less. Resentment seethed and in 1981 rioting returned to the streets of Liverpool. Hundreds were injured as rioters hurled petrol bombs and bricks at the police, and television viewers watched in disbelief as

A solicitors' office destroyed by petrol bombs during the Toxteth riots.

Another stark example of the aftermath of the riots.

scenes reminiscent of the Belfast riots of the 1960s and '70s were re-enacted on their screens. Toxteth now enjoys the dubious honour of being the scene of the very first ever use of CS gas for riot control on the British mainland.

And it wasn't only television viewers who were shocked. The Tory government at last realised that a policy of *laissez-faire* was no longer an option. Action was needed yesterday. Mrs Thatcher, finally realising that the Scousers had reached the end of their tether, appointed Michael Heseltine as Minister for Merseyside and dispatched him to the north-west to take charge of a situation which was growing uglier by the minute. All of a sudden money was found to lavish on the area in a massive makeover exercise. The city was spruced up in what seemed like no time at all; the derelict land around the docks was miraculously converted into the venue for the International Garden Festival, opened by the Queen and Duke of Edinburgh in 1984. To Liverpudlians trying to live on the dole, such 'tarting up' might have seemed like too little too late, but at least it was a start. It was the beginning of the slow climb back up the economic hill, and as the economic situation in the country as a whole began to improve, so did Liverpool's.

But the history of Liverpool in the last fifty years has not all been doom and gloom. There have been pockets of success, activity, drive and innovation which have given Liverpool a national and international reputation for talent and creative genius.

Williamson Square in 1946. No double yellow lines or parking meters in those days!

Church Street in the 1930s. (Sutton Collection)

As ever, despite financial and social problems, Liverpool continued to build and construction was not confined to replacing the old with the new or the bomb damaged with the pristine. In the 1960s, additions continued to be made to the skyline as the city seemed to build ever upwards in a symbolic demonstration of masculine vigour, proclaiming to the whole world that Liverpool still had a lot to offer and those who thought the city was dead were in for a shock. A brand new Liverpool was about to burst onto the scene in a way which few could have foreseen and even fewer would have dared to predict.

The decades of the post-war re-vamp saw major building projects all over Liverpool and particularly in the city centre. The area including Williamson Square, the old St John's Market, Clayton Square and Parker Street was completely re-styled and re-built. The original Georgian layout was totally transformed and the rather dingy shops and offices were replaced with bright, airy modern buildings which now give that part of the city centre a fresh, clean look. Looming over the whole scene is the 450ft St John's Beacon whose crowning glory was once a revolving restaurant which, for a few short years, gave Liverpool's sophisticated diners the opportunity

St John's shopping mall replaced the original market (opened 1822) where Cilla Black's mother once had a stall.

A completely transformed Williamson Square as it appeared in 2007.

Clayton Square shopping centre: a bright, modern replacement for the dingy old shops and news theatre that used to occupy this site.

St John's Beacon as seen from Williamson Square.

St John's Beacon as seen from Mount Pleasant.

of looking out onto an ever-changing panoramic view of the city as they ate their prawn cocktails and T-bone steaks. Now it houses the radio stations Radio City and Magic 1548.

The other major building project of the era was the Catholic Cathedral. With the arrival of Irish immigrants in the 1840s, the vast majority of whom were Catholic, it was felt that Liverpool needed a cathedral to cater for their spiritual needs. A suitable site was chosen in Everton and an architect, Edward Pugin, was commissioned for the task. But the project never got beyond the drawing board stage, as the church authorities soon realised that a cathedral would be something of an expensive luxury when there was an even more pressing need to provide schools, churches and orphanages for the comfort and succour of the homeless and destitute children of the parish.

But the idea did not die; it was merely allowed to sleep for a while. It was awakened again in the 1920s although it was not until 1930 that a new site was chosen, and this time it was a mere few hundred yards from the Anglican Cathedral. Sir Edward Lutyens was then offered the commission to design a building that would rival its Anglican counterpart, which had been progressing steadily since 1904. He accepted the challenge and produced a plan for a massive

The Catholic Cathedral with its somewhat eccentric belfry.

structure with a great dome 168ft in diameter and an internal height of 300ft. The high alter was to be 12ft above the nave floor and the nave, transept, apses and sacristies were to be lined with no fewer than fifty-three altars. In other words the building, had it been built, would have dwarfed the Anglican Cathedral when it too was eventually finished.

At first it looked as if everything would go to plan, and work actually started on the new cathedral. But then war broke out, and, although building continued until 1941, by which time the crypt was almost completed, the decision was taken to suspend all construction work until the cessation of hostilities, whenever that would be. When building did restart it was only for time enough to finish the crypt. The cost of completing the whole project had risen to an unbelievable and totally unattainable £27,000,000. It was a case of 'down tools' for at least the foreseeable future, and many thought forever.

In 1960, Archbishop John Carmel Heenan decided it was time to make another attempt. He organised a worldwide competition in which architects were invited to submit plans for a cathedral, taking the existing crypt as their starting point. Sir Frederick Gibberd's (1908–84) design was declared the winner and building began in October 1962. In May 1965 the job was complete and the new cathedral consecrated.

Its official title is the Metropolitan Cathedral of Christ the King although it is more colloquially referred to, because of its strange, vaguely conical shape, as Paddy's Wigwam or the Mersey Funnel. And the rather eccentric outer design is matched by an equally unusual inner layout. The traditional longitudinal shape we normally associate with cathedrals and churches is dispensed with almost entirely. What the visitor is now confronted with as he passes through the magnificent portal is virtually guaranteed to be something of a shock to the system. There is a circular arrangement of the pews where worshippers gaze down onto a centrally positioned altar so that the whole impact is reminiscent more of an ancient Greek amphitheatre than of our traditional view of a church. Those who commissioned and designed the building believed that such an arrangement would allow the congregation (up to 2,000 in number) to feel more involved with the proceedings. In traditional cathedrals and churches the altar and clergyman appear very distant, in both senses, from the congregation. In Frederick Gibberd's Metropolitan Cathedral, the architecture is designed to give the impression that the priest and congregation are worshipping together; the more traditional design tends to make this feeling of involvement very difficult. Also, the futuristic architecture can be seen as a figurative sloughing off of the more unpleasant aspects of the past and an anticipation of a future in which the prejudices and bitterness between Catholic and Protestant can be forgotten. And this symbolism is reinforced by the accidentally apt symbolism of the two cathedrals' position; they are less than half a mile away from each other and joined by Hope Street.

Along with the rebuilding of offices and public buildings, of course, there was also an urgent need to build places where people could live. The bombing, demobilisation and the ever-present problem of slum clearance meant that decent housing with proper facilities became priority number one. As a short-term, stop-gap measure to alleviate the most pressing difficulties the government opted for a massive programme of erecting 'pre-fabs', or 'pre-fabricated homes' which were mass-produced in factories and then transported to the construction sites where they were assembled. The huge advantage of such a system was that reasonably decent accommodation (with bathrooms, in-built fridges and often a little garden!) could be provided for people at a reasonable cost and in a fraction of the time that more traditional methods of construction would require. On the other hand, these buildings were constructed mainly of steel and corrugated asbestos cement and consequently were very difficult to heat. There was no such thing as central heating or double glazing and as the pre-fab walls were no more than a few centimetres thick, it was almost impossible for the inhabitants to keep warm in winter, no matter how much coal was heaped on the fire.

In order to provide a more lasting solution to the problem, Liverpool Corporation embarked on a programme of house building on the city's periphery in places such as Huyton, Kirkby and Speke. To a certain extent this was not a new scheme but merely the resurrection of the slum clearance programme of the 1930s, although

A scene from a Kirkby housing estate.

now the sense of urgency was somewhat greater. And of all the new estates that sprang up during this period, Kirkby's was the most spectacular. Until the town planners decided that this was the ideal place for their grand designs, Kirkby had been little more than a sleepy Lancashire village. It was mentioned as 'Cherchbi' in the Domesday Book, and before the bulldozers arrived in 1952 its population still had not exceeded 3,000. But by 1965 its population had reached 52,000! Such a growth rate was unmatched anywhere else in the country.

When the planners turned their attention to the housing problems closer to the city centre, where land was very much at a premium, the new byword was 'maximum density' housing. This, in effect, meant building high-rise flats and maisonettes (i.e. two-storey flats) in towers blocks, sometimes twelve or fifteen storeys high. They proved to be an unmitigated disaster. The planners seemed not to realise that forcing people into such 'piggeries', as those on Netherfield Road came to be known, would have dreadful practical, social and psychological effects. The planners did what Hitler never managed to do: they destroyed the community spirit that united those who lived in the old terraced houses. Gone were the days when housewives could chat to each other as they 'donkey-stoned' the front step; gone were the days when their menfolk could take a chair out onto the pavement on a fine summer evening and enjoy a smoke and some friendly banter with the neighbour across the street. Gone also were the days when the banter could lead to neighbours enjoying a bottle or two of beer together as they sat outside and watched the sun disappear behind the cranes and derricks in the Birkenhead shipyards.

What was on offer now to the residents of Liverpool was a very different lifestyle. Mothers could no longer keep a watchful eye on their children as they played hopscotch or football in the road (there were fewer cars then!). People lived literally in the clouds, unable to let their kids out by themselves; older folk found the gangs of youths who liked to gather on the stairwells intimidating, and everyday tasks such as shopping became a major problem. If the lifts were working, transporting a couple of shopping bags up ten floors was not too much of a problem, but if they were out of action, as was frequently the case, even the young were fit to drop by the time they reached their front door. Less able-bodied and older residents were forced to stay indoors for much of the time as something as simple as popping out to post a letter became a nightmare involving forward planning of almost military proportions. People became prisoners in their own homes and the next generation of planners was forced to do some serious re-thinking.

But there were also changes of another kind afoot in the 1960s. The austerity of the post-war years was giving way to Harold McMillan's 'you've never had it so good' years and people found that they had a bit more money in their pockets. The younger generation in particular was now asserting itself in a way which previous generations had been unable or unwilling to do. The parents could still remember the war and many were still suffering from its aftermath, but for the younger generation Adolf Hitler was just somebody the history teacher talked about and then you wrote an essay about for homework. Reality for the Liverpool teenagers in the late 1950s and early '60s was the latest in hairstyles, Italian suits, hooped skirts, coffee bars and, increasingly, foreign holidays.

And there was also something else: music. The influence of American popular music had always been strong and this was particularly noticeable after the war. In the 1950s, American singers such as Johnny Ray, Slim Whitman, Frankie Lane, Frank Sinatra and, of course, Elvis Presley, and a host of others had enjoyed great popularity in Liverpool as in the rest of the country. In fact, so great was their influence that it was a brave youngster with showbiz ambitions who did not model himself on one of the American idols. British singers such as Cliff Richard, Billy Fury (a Liverpool lad) and Marty Wilde all copied their counterparts across the Atlantic, particularly Elvis. The huge quiff, the slick, swept-back hair and sideburns were de rigueur for any aspiring pop singer as was the ability to curl the mouth up at one side while trying to look all sultry and sound like 'the King'. And, of course, you had to have a guitar.

The entrance into The Cavern, 2007.

Presumably John Lennon in effigy.

Then it all changed. Almost overnight America was no longer the centre of the pop universe; Liverpool was. And the epicentre of this universe was the dingy basement of an old fruit warehouse in a miserable little side street not far from the commercial centre of the city. The miserable side street was Mathew Street (for some reason spelt with only one 't') and the dingy basement was, of course, The Cavern.

Since 1957 this warehouse cellar had been the venue for local jazz bands (it took its name from the jazz club in Paris called Le Caveau) and had hosted performances by such as the late George Melly, The Merseysippi Jazz Band and other famous bands whose names haunt the pages of lengthy tomes devoted to the history of the genre. But then, by the early '60s, the walls of the three arches comprising the cellar were resounding to the music of a very different sort. Four young local lads who originally styled themselves The Quarrymen (taking their name from Quarry Bank, the grammar school where the lead singer, John Lennon, had been a pupil) but had now transmogrified into The Beatles, began to make more and more frequent appearances and their rock'n'roll music eventually came to dominate the scene as the jazz bands found themselves increasingly pushed onto the sidelines. And their impact was not confined to the music. Yes, they were in the process of squeezing out jazz and simultaneously showing the wider pop world that the days of the American crooners and pop idols were also numbered, but their influence was to be felt in other spheres as well. Liverpool's turn had come and The Beatles were about to take the country and the whole world by storm. Guided by the genius of their manager Brian Epstein, they introduced new concepts that cut across the whole spectrum of cultural activity not only for their generation but for generations to come. They dominated fashion; out went the quiff and swept-back hair and in came the monkish hairstyle (minus the tonsure!) which was The Beatles' trademark: hair brushed forward into a fringe without a glint of hair cream or gel in sight. Next came the suits with no lapels and high, rounded collars. The pop world had seen nothing like it, but from 1962, when the group had their first hit record 'Love me do', no pop group would dare to even appear on stage with hairstyles and suits that did not emulate The Beatles to a greater rather than a lesser degree.

The success enjoyed by The Beatles is now legendary, as is that enjoyed by many other groups and individual singers who were carried along on the crest of the wave created by John, Paul, George and Ringo. Cilla Black, Gerry and the Pacemakers, the Merseybeats, and many, many more, all found a place in Liverpool's Hall of Fame because they had the talent, the drive and the luck to be where they were when they were.

It wasn't only the singers who did well. This was also a time when other forms of creativity seemed to blossom in Liverpool and not least among them was poetry. While John Lennon and his ilk were churning out songs for their respective groups, Liverpudlians such as Roger McGough, Brian Patten and Adrian Henri were quickly gaining a reputation for themselves as poets. And the poetry they produced was much appreciated by the generation that had been fed (in some cases, force-fed) lines penned by such worthies as Shakespeare, Byron, Wordsworth and Keats. Roger McGough et al. offered something new: poetry that was relevant, lively, imaginative and experimental. It was writing which Liverpudlians, particularly of the younger generation, could appreciate because it dealt with themes they did not find in the Classics: the Bomb, sex, politics, etc. And its style was fresh and easily accessible. The poetry of the Liverpool poets was rapid, full of word play, linguistic experimentation and a combination of Surrealism and Impressionism. It mixed humour with pathos, originality with verve. In brief it was poetry that was fun. But perhaps most importantly it was poetry that was meant to be read out to live audiences, not studied and dissected in dry, academically pretentious essays or discussed during soporific lectures and seminars. These poets wanted to make people think about contemporary issues, and the best way to reach their intended audience was to read their works aloud in pubs, jazz clubs, The Cavern and at pop concerts. And some of them, nearly fifty years later, are still doing it.

Then there's the branch of Liverpool culture without which no history of the city, however brief, would be complete: football. So ingrained in the civic psyche of Liverpool is the game that for many people the world over the words 'Liverpool' and 'football' are almost synonymous. The importance of the game for Liverpudlians is such that the old Scouse joke about the Liver Building needing two Liver Birds, one to watch the river and the other to watch the football, could almost be true.

Football has done a lot for Liverpool and for Liverpudlians. In the post-war years anticipation of Saturday's match provided a powerful antidote to the cash-strapped, hand-to-mouth existence still led by many people. The difficulties of making ends meet from Monday to Friday (in fact, for most people in those days the working week finished at noon on Saturday) could be forgotten on a Saturday afternoon at either Goodison or Anfield watching the 'toffees' (Everton) or the 'reds' (Liverpool).

The therapeutic benefits of watching football did not end there: on Saturday nights pubs throughout the city would be filled with ardent supporters reliving the day's match, and for a few hours all the cares of the world evaporated in a haze of cigarette smoke seen through the bottom of an upturned beer glass. While dads were at work in the week, the kids would come home from school and kick a ball about in the street or on the waste ground of a cleared bombsite, seeing themselves as Billy Liddell, Albert Stubbins or the legendary goalkeepers, Tommy

You just can't get away from football in Liverpool! This stall is one of several selling soccer paraphernalia in the city centre.

Younger and Ted Sagar. With their short trousers, bruised knees and mucky faces they imagined themselves scoring magnificent goals and making brilliant saves in front of a capacity crowd of appreciative fans; the dream only ended when their mums called them in for tea.

Organised football came to Merseyside in 1878 when the lads from St Domingo's Methodist Church in Everton decided to put their weekly kickabouts onto a more formal footing. The result was a team rejoicing in the name of St Domingo's FC, but a year later it was decided, for some obscure reason, that the team should change its name and so, in 1878, it became Everton FC. At almost the same time, the players acquired the nickname 'the toffees' in honour of the wonderful delicacies known as Everton Toffees, produced in that part of Liverpool since the 1750s to what for many years was a jealously guarded secret recipe.

Within a relatively short time this team of what we might justifiably refer to as a collection of enthusiastic amateurs were becoming quite formidable as opponents on the football field, and when the Football League was founded in 1888, Everton was one of the first teams to be included. In the 1890/91 season the team won the League championship, as they did again in 1914/15, having also won the FA Cup in 1905/6.

When the directors then signed on a young local player called William Dean in 1925, even they probably did not realise what a gem they had. Young Dean, a native of Birkenhead, was playing for Tranmere Rovers at the time and Everton had to pay the magnificent sum of £3,000 for his services, which in those days would have been an enormous amount. But the money was not wasted and Billy Dean (or Dixie as his fans christened him because his dark complexion and curly black hair made him look like someone from America's Deep South) did his new team proud. He was a brilliant all-round footballer and could shoot, tackle and dribble with the best of them. But his outstanding talent was in the air; his ability to head a ball powerfully and accurately was simply way beyond anything the football world had ever seen. His skills are still talked about today in the world of football, and the record he set of sixty goals in thirty-nine league games (the 1927/8 season) has never been equalled, let alone beaten.

In the early years the team played on a pitch occupying a corner of Stanley Park but soon moved to the ground we now associate with another Merseyside club, Anfield, where it remained until 1892. Then there was an argument with the landlord over rent and the team packed its bags and moved further down the road to Goodison Park, the ground which has been Everton's home ever since. Meanwhile, back at Anfield, it was decided that another team should be formed up and this new side was to be known as Liverpool FC. And this has been the arrangement ever since: Liverpool at Anfield and Everton at Goodison.

Liverpool's early days were not crowned with the success Everton had enjoyed almost right from the start. In fact, Liverpool had a disastrous first season and at the end of it was relegated to the Second Division. But, to their credit, they showed grit and determination and within a year had not only fought their way back to the First

Memorial to the Liverpool boys who fell during the Boer War.

Division but ended the season in fifth place, higher up the leader board than Everton who were now becoming their great rivals.

The first time they won the championship was in 1900/1, but the euphoria was short-lived; two years later they were relegated again, only to come back fighting yet again and win their second championship in the 1904/5 season. This time their resilience was rewarded by the directors, who made the wonderfully magnanimous gesture of building a raised terrace for the fans to give them a better view of future games. In honour of those brave Liverpool lads who had gone off to fight in the Boer War and had never returned, the terrace was named Spion Kop after the scene of the battle in South Africa in January 1900 where 8,000 Boers defeated 20,000 British troops. 'The Kop' and 'The Kop Choir', with its signature tune 'You'll never walk alone', are known to football fans throughout the world even today.

Spionkop

This is often explained as being an Afrikaans expression but in actual fact it is Dutch and the Afrikaans spelling would be 'spoeionkop'.

The confusion arises from the similarity between the two languages; Afrikaans is a form of Dutch which evolved among the Dutch settlers in South Africa, known as the Boers, a word which simply means 'farmers' in Dutch. Although it is spelt as one word in both Afrikaans and Dutch, the English prefer to spell it as two.

'Spionkop' is literally 'Spy Hill' and was so-called because it offered the Boers a vantage point from which to observe enemy troops movements

Everton and Liverpool Football Clubs have both enjoyed long and more or less successful careers in the history of the game, although, of course, they have had their days of disappointment as well as their days of glory. Unfortunately, Liverpool has also had its days of grief, although it has to be said that when the news of the desperately tragic events at Heysel and Hillsborough filtered through, the tears shed in the city were not confined to supporters of just one team. A sense of horror and disbelief gripped the whole city; Liverpool supporters, Everton supporters and even people who had no interest in football were stunned by the news.

At the Heysel Stadium in Belgium, Liverpool were playing against Juventus in the 1985 European Cup final when fighting broke out between rival fans. In the mêlée a wall collapsed and thirty-eight Juventus fans were killed. Juventus won the match and Liverpool had to return home, not only as the losing side, but bearing much of the blame for what had happened. As a result, all English clubs were banned from taking part in European football indefinitely.

Then, in 1989, yet another tragedy struck. This time Liverpool were playing Nottingham Forest at Hillsborough with the Leppings Lane end of the stand was filled to capacity and more and more fans still tried to get in to see the match. Some of those at the front overflowed onto the pitch in a desperate attempt to escape the crush. Most managed to reach safety but ninety-six Liverpool spectators were crushed to death. This was without doubt the blackest day in the history of football on Merseyside.

The ups and downs of Liverpool and Everton football teams in many ways mirror the history of Liverpool itself. Football, like the city, grew from humble beginnings. It went on to enjoy rapid grown and enormous success and then suffered setbacks and reversals, but the fans, just as those who live and work in the city, remained loyal and never gave up on their teams. The silverware brought home to Goodison and Anfield may not have been as plentiful as the fans would have liked, but the teams are still among the best in the world and show every sign of remaining such. There can be no better example of Liverpool's grit and determination than the team's unbelievable win against AC Milan in the final of the European Cup in 2005; the match will be talked about, written about and read about for generations to come.

By half-time, many of the fans, disgusted with Liverpool's poor performance which resulted in their being 3–0 down at half time, had left the stadium assuming that it was all over and the Reds were in for a humiliating defeat. But the Gods were on Liverpool's side and the team fought back to an amazing 3–3 score when the final whistle blew. In the shoot-out that followed, the Merseyside giants won 3–2 and for the fifth time in their history, Liverpool FC were European Champions.

Meanwhile, elsewhere . . .

1947   Marriage of Princess Elizabeth to Prince Philip of Greece
1956   British and French troops occupied Suez Canal
1959   The first section of the M1 motorway opened
1965   Death penalty abolished in Britain
1971   Decimal coinage introduced
1973   Britain joined the Common Market
1982   Falklands War between Britain and Argentina
1994   Channel Tunnel opened
2004   Fox hunting with hounds banned in England and Wales
2005   Terrorists bombed the London Underground
2006   Saddam Hussein, ex-President of Iraq was executed
2007   Gordon Brown became Prime Minister

The city of Liverpool, then, has seen it all. From its inauspicious beginnings 800 years ago it has grown into one of the major cities in the world and has been nominated as Capital of Culture for 2008. It has seen joy, tragedy, success and failure, but it has never ceased to be itself. It has engendered a rare breed of citizen: tough, businesslike, gritty and yet with a ready wit and sense of humour almost unequalled anywhere in the rest of the country. Its situation on the banks of the Mersey has given the city a history which inevitably benefited from its links, not only with its nearest neighbour, Wales, and also Ireland, but with the rest of the world.

The result is a proud, modern city, a 'come-back-kid' among the towns and cities of Britain. And, as if to demonstrate the city's continuing ability to grow and to assert itself, an ambitious redevelopment of the city centre was begun in October 2004. At a cost of £800,000,000, the area around Paradise Street is to be converted into a glistening, futuristically-designed shopping-cum-leisure precinct for the delight of Liverpudlians and visitors alike. The intention is that by the time the city assumes the role of Capital of Culture in 2008, one of the most run-down areas of the city will have been transformed into a spanking brand-new showpiece of modern urban living. There will be new shops, hotels, and a cinema, and the whole development will be crowned with a city-centre park covering an area of five-and-a-half acres, and much of the new development will engulf that part of Liverpool where it all began all those centuries ago. The little fishing hamlet that caught King John's eye in

Plaque on the wall of the Flanagan's Apple pub in Mathew Street, just a few yards from The Cavern.

the thirteenth century is still very much alive and kicking in the twenty-first. Small wonder, then, that the eminent psychologist Carl Jung, after a dream that he had visited Liverpool in 1927, was able to claim that, 'Liverpool is the pool of life'.

BIBLIOGRAPHY

BOOKS

Anon, *Liverpool and Slavery*, Bowker & Son, 1884
Aughton, Peter, *Liverpool: A People's History*, Carnegie Publishing Ltd, 2003
Belcham, John (Ed.), *Liverpool 800*, Liverpool University Press, 2006
Chandler, George, *Liverpool*, B.T. Batsford Ltd, 1957
Channon, Howard, *Portrait of Liverpool*, Robert Hale and Co., 1070
Charters, David, *Liverpool: The world in one city*, Bluecoat Press, 2003
Fletcher, Mike, *The Making of Liverpool*, Wharncliffe Books, 2004
Harding, Stephen, *Viking Mersey*, Countyvise Ltd, 2002
Horton, Steven, *Street Names of the City of Liverpool*, Countyvise Ltd, 2002
Lewis, David, *Walks through History: Liverpool*, Breedon Books, 2004
Morgan, Kenneth O., *Oxford Illustrated History of Britain*, OUP, 1989
Miller, John, *The Stuarts*, Hambledon Continuum, 2004
Muir, Ramsay, *A History of Liverpool*, Liverpool University Press, 1907
Perret, Bryan, *Liverpool: A City at War*, Hugo Press, 2005
Porter, Roy, *English Society in the Eighteenth Century*, Penguin Books, 1991
Ross, David, *England, History of a Nation*, Geddes and Crosset, 2005
Sharples, Joseph, *Liverpool*, Yale University Press, 2004
Whynne-Hammond, Charles, *English Place Names Explained*,
  Countryside Books, 2005

WEBSITES

Mike Royden's local history pages – www.roydenhistory.co.uk
www.localhistories.org/liverpool
www.bbc.co.uk/liverpool/localhistory

ACKNOWLEDGEMENTS

There are several people whom I have to thank for the valuable assistance they gave me during the preparation of this volume.

Roger Hull, David Stokey and their colleagues at the Liverpool Record Office were a great help in providing the answers to questions I had about Liverpool's history and locating many of the drawings and photographs which, hopefully, add interest to this book. I am particularly grateful to the staff of Liverpool Record Office for allowing me to use its translation of King John's original Charter as it appears in the introduction.

I am no less indebted to Mr Paul Murray of the Sea Life Centre at Rhyl, Mark Ives of the Centre for Environment, Fisheries and Aquaculture Science in Lowestoft and Mr Keith West-Adams of Whitstable in Kent, for sharing their encyclopaedic knowledge of fishing with me and confirming my doubts about salmon thriving, or indeed surviving, in a 'clogged' pool.

Last, but by no means least, I would like to thank my wife Jean for her encouragement and support and for coming up with helpful suggestions on several occasions when I was gripped by the dreaded 'writer's block'.